BEHIND THE CURTAIN

BEHIND
THE CURTAIN

INSIDE THE NETWORK OF PROGRESSIVE BILLIONAIRES
AND THEIR CAMPAIGN TO UNDERMINE DEMOCRACY

JEFF REYNOLDS

BOMBARDIER
B O O K S

A BOMBARDIER BOOKS BOOK
An Imprint of Post Hill Press

Behind the Curtain:
Inside the Network of Progressive Billionaires
and Their Campaign to Undermine Democracy
© 2019 by Jeff Reynolds
All Rights Reserved

ISBN: 978-1-68261-707-6
ISBN (eBook): 978-1-68261-708-3

Cover design by Christian Bentulan and Cody Corcoran

Post Hill Press
New York • Nashville
posthillpress.com

Published in the United States of America

TABLE OF CONTENTS

INTRODUCTION

"Journalism is printing what someone else does not want printed; everything else is public relations."

—GEORGE ORWELL

Prior to Election Day 2016, very few Americans had heard of Antifa. Their grand entrée into America's consciousness played out across television screens for several weeks in November and December of 2016. In cities all over the East Coast and West Coast, they looted, they rioted, they blocked freeways, they destroyed property, they committed arson—and they claimed grassroots legitimacy from behind black masks. They protested because Donald Trump won the contest to become America's 45th president.

Of course, living in the belly of the beast—ultra-liberal Portland, Oregon—I had heard of Antifa. This is the town that George H. W. Bush once called Little Beirut.[1] We see a lot of action here. Antifa's overt actions to destroy the First Amendment included alliances with veteran anarchists who utilized Black Bloc tactics in the 1999 Battle of Seattle, Occupy Portland protesters (and Occupy groups across the nation), Black Lives Matter, By Any Means Necessary, and a whole host of other violent activist groups on the radical left.[2] Portland's Antifa goons frequently take road trips to Seattle, Berkeley, Oakland, and other hot spots on the Left Coast to participate in violent and destructive riots. They use such violent means to intimidate their enemies into giving up their rights to free speech. In an opinion piece for *The Hill*, for example, Johnathan Turley cites several examples in which Antifa members expressed their desire to shut down free speech for Republicans, conservatives, and anyone else they deem to be fascists:

> "At Berkeley and other universities, protesters have held up signs saying 'F--k Free Speech' and have threatened to beat up anyone taking their pictures, including journalists. They seem blissfully ignorant of the contradiction in using fascistic tactics as anti-fascist protesters. After all, a leading definition of fascism is 'a tendency toward or actual exercise of strong autocratic or dictatorial control.'
>
> "CNN recently interviewed antifa protesters who insist that violence is simply the language that their opponents understand. Leftist organizer Scott Crow endorsed illegal actions and said that antifa activists cover their faces to 'avoid the ramifications of law enforcement.' Such violent logic is supported by some professors.
>
> "Last week, Clemson University Professor Bart Knijnenburg went on Facebook to call Trump supporters and Republicans 'racist scum.' He added, 'I admire anyone who stands up against white supremacy, violent or nonviolent. This needs to stop, by any means necessary. #PunchNazis.'

He is not alone. Trinity College Professor Johnny Williams, who teaches classes on race, posted attacks on bigots and called on people to 'let them f-----g die.'"[3]

Such a determination requires little more than disagreement with their ideology. While they have taken on prominent controversial targets and alt-right provocateurs, they also cast a wide net.

That net ensnared my fellow volunteers and me in April 2017, when Antifa targeted the Avenue of Roses Parade in Northeast Portland. As a former chair of the Multnomah County Republican Party in Portland, I stay involved, and I had a front-row seat. Having participated in this event for several years prior, we did not anticipate any problems with our parade entry. Dozens of volunteers—parents, grandparents, members of the community—watched in frustration as Antifa-aligned anarchist groups threatened and intimidated the parade organizers over the Republican Party entry. The two Antifa-affiliated groups, Oregon Students United and Direct Action Alliance, created counterprotest events to encourage activists to confront individual Republicans directly.[4]

Then things really got out of hand. One activist anonymously emailed the parade organizers to let them know that their protest would not be peaceful. The email stated, "We will have two hundred or more people rush into the parade into the middle and drag and push those people out.... You have seen how much power we have downtown and that the police cannot stop us from shutting down roads so please consider your decision wisely."[5]

The last sentence, bragging about the police not being able to stop them, refers to the riots that besieged Portland for several days in November 2016. Violence had recently been visited upon the city, and residents were fearful and weary.

Buckling under the pressure of a credible threat of violence, The Rose City Business Alliance and the Portland Rose Festival Foundation chose to cancel the parade outright, despite assurances from the Portland Police Bureau that sufficient police personnel were available to handle safety and security concerns. I know this because I spoke personally with Pete Simpson, the spokesman for the bureau. He assured me that parade organizers were told sufficient officers from the East Precinct could have been made available for security, with officers from the Central Precinct also available as backup.

Incidentally, a rather interesting article dropped in the Daily Caller in April 2017, after students and rioters at the University of California at Berkeley shut down the campus and burned stuff in response to an adult guest lecturer presenting worldviews with which they didn't agree. Titled, "Documents Tie Berkeley Riot Organizers To Pro-Pedophilia Group, NAMBLA," the article demonstrates that the Antifa-affiliated direct action group By Any Means Necessary (BAMN) has direct ties to the North American Man/Boy Love Association (NAMBLA), which advocates in favor of pedophilia rights.[6] The DC reports BAMN was founded by a small communist organization in Detroit, the Revolutionary Workers League (RWL). NAMBLA documents from a 1991 conference show the RWL as a supporting organization, endorsing "gay rights in general and NAMBLA in particular." Who are the founders of BAMN, who helped make the Berkeley riots extra violent? The DC writes, "Shanta Driver...BAMN's founder and co-chair, was affiliated with RWL as early as 1983, according to the *Workers Vanguard*, a communist publication. She also identified herself to the *Los Angeles Times* as an activist with RWL in late 1995 while protesting in Berkeley. Driver's former law partner, Eileen Scheff—who has represented BAMN on multiple occasions, including at the Supreme Court—has been a self-described 'member of NAMBLA.' The bulletin identified Scheff as an RWL member."

Nice company those rioters keep.

The Election Day riots in 2016 had victimized the city of Portland in an unchecked reign of terror just a few months prior.[7] Liberal Portland was upset and on edge over the rejection of Hillary Clinton at the polls, and the election of Donald Trump as president. Many residents wanted an outlet to vent their fears and frustrations in peaceful demonstrations. Antifa thugs joined the #Resist protests, nudging them into violent acts. Protesters destroyed dozens of vehicles at a car dealership. A wave of hundreds of rioters took to the interstate freeways several nights in a row, bringing traffic to a halt and causing chaos for motorists. One pregnant woman driving home from work was sent into a panic, but 911 operators were unable to send timely assistance due to the traffic jam.[8] Marchers illegally blocked city streets, broke windows and doors, looted shops, and set things on fire.

I've witnessed, firsthand, the worst of the resistance.

This episode displayed some of the extremes to which the most radical leftists will go to join the resistance. Many of the boots on the ground protesters, dismayed that Hillary lost to The Donald and wanting to #Resist, were unaware of the thugs who would try to hijack the protests and deliberately turn them violent. If one looks hard enough at these protests, one sees the hidden interconnections between groups assumed to be organic, bottom-up, grassroots uprisings. Few Americans watching the resistance unfold, or participating in #Resist themselves, have any awareness of just how deeply the connections intertwine with establishment Democrats, Wall Street players, billionaire mega-donors, dirty money, and forces that wish to undermine the American concept of personal liberty. They think that joining Indivisible or wearing a pink pussy hat means they participate in an organic uprising. Instead, participation in these groups serves little more than advancing the corporatist framework they despise. The billionaire puppet masters and their specially chosen ringleaders want this to remain secret, so they can play both sides—peaceful demonstrators and nonprofits on one side, violent rioters and a splintering society on the other.

These shameless attempts to co-opt peaceful protests continue unabated to this day. One need look no further than the takeover of the Student Walkout movement in favor of gun control in the wake of the Parkland, Florida, school shooting. It didn't take long to reveal that the #MarchForOurLives national school walkouts were taken over and coordinated by the Women's March movement, Moms Demand Action (a gun control group), Planned Parenthood, and a whole host of other radical organizations.[9, 10]

Despite appearances, Antifa does not exist in a vacuum, nor is it a utopian revolution of thousands of young people desperately clamoring for capitalism to be destroyed. This is deliberate subterfuge. The loose affiliation of aligned groups prefers it to remain this way, and so does the dark money that keeps them alive. After all, it might undermine the message to reveal that somebody is paying these activists to protest. More than one Uber driver has told me that protesters they had as passengers in 2016 and 2017 openly bragged about being paid and traveling to Portland from Seattle or some other location. They bragged about being told by organizers that they already had enough protesters in Seattle, so they were being sent to Portland to bolster the numbers in our streets. A cursory search of the internet returns all sorts of evidence of paid liberal protesters, as well as employers who will pay workers for their activism.[11, 12, 13, 14]

Many readers might be familiar with the common practice of unions busing members to other states to support local strikers. For instance, New York Teamsters sent a small army of members to Wisconsin in 2011 to add to the large number of protesters that took over the Capitol after Governor Scott Walker's pension reform bills passed.[15] Few are aware that most of the groups in the resistance get large injections of cash for their operations from the same sources—public worker unions, dark money from anonymous billionaires, and nonprofits that move their money around to hide the original sources.

Those being paid to riot, and those who pay them, would really rather you just don't know about their little arrangement. The same goes for Black Lives Matter, Indivisible, the #Resist movement, Occupy Wall Street and their local affiliates, and scores of teacher union and public sector union strikes across the nation over the past several years. Busloads of protesters magically appear and ramp up the rhetoric and the actions of a local protest. Where do they come from? Why are they there? Who are they working with? Most importantly, who's paying their expenses?

A shadowy underworld of the ultra-rich and ultra-activist pulls the strings in the puppet show of street protests. These campaigns don't simply spring up out of civil unrest. Protesters don't just magically appear and start breaking windows, setting cars on fire, or terrorizing motorists on freeways. These campaigns are created, tested, measured, refined, and funded away from the prying eyes of the press by a sort of league of leftist mega-donors. They push these pet campaigns and these protests by taking advantage of the tax codes of the Internal Revenue Service that govern nonprofit organizations and their activities. Funding an endless array of interconnected nonprofit groups allows them to maintain a high degree of anonymity, while presenting themselves as patrons of the philanthropic world. The foundations claim altruistic goals: educating the public about the environment, advocating for racial equality, fighting for governmental transparency, strengthening democracy across the world, supporting independent investigative journalism, pushing for world peace, urging nuclear non-proliferation, fighting hate crime, and a host of other causes in an appeal to our higher calling. These interconnected nonprofits, using some designation of educational or social service organization, pass money back and forth. These organizations give one another grants, they use one another to scrub the original donor of responsibility for the organizations and their activities, and they enrich an army of organizational executives and fundraisers who take their cut every step along the way. Additionally, the deeper one investigates, the more it becomes evident that the movement includes folks who would cause embarrassment—and possible legal inquiries—if their activities and relationships were to come to light.

When someone goes to such lengths to hide their associations, generally a good reason exists. In too many instances, donors and activists associate with the types of unsavory people who do not generate positive public relations. In many cases, these schemes to shield donors from scrutiny appear to be Federal Election Commission (FEC) complaints waiting to happen.

This cabal of super-donors is made up of several individuals who made their money by enthusiastically participating in our free market economy. The great irony of their philanthropy later in life is that their donations often fund groups that make it harder for others to enjoy the success they had in their careers. Hedge fund managers who enjoy fantastic wealth beyond comprehension will fund organizations that promote a greatly expanded regulatory state, higher taxes, interference in the wage markets, outside demands on the conditions of employment such as mandatory sick time and maternity time—in short, a command economy to replace the free market. Organizations that explicitly take advantage of the new reality of independent expenditure rules created by the *Citizens United v. Federal Election Commission* decision work diligently at several levels to shackle the First Amendment rights of every citizen. Many of the great industrialists of the twentieth century set up foundations to manage the wealth they created and donate it to charitable causes, but those foundations—and the people who run them—often fund efforts diametrically opposed to the intentions of their founders.

It goes beyond that. Follow the money. In many cases, these mega-donors have no intention of doing anything differently in their philanthropic lives than they did while actively creating their fantastic wealth. Investors invest their money to make a profit. Philanthropy, sadly, often boils down to a cynical desire for a return on investment, with the added benefit of improving the public image of the philanthropist. The easiest way to get there is by simple reductions in their taxable income—a deduction for a charitable donation. They can also accomplish this by influencing public policy in a way that is friendlier to a particular politician's financial backer and that creates an artificial, government-created and -supported monopoly, or by gaming the markets with governmental interference designed to produce a particular result, allowing investors to participate in government-aided insider trading.

These returns on investment require a grand trust exercise among supporters of the movement who end up suspending disbelief like they would in a movie theater. In order to create momentum, grassroots supporters have to believe that the cause is just. Environmentalists and social justice warriors and community organizers and other activists on the Left, in order to trust the movement, have to know with certitude that the motivations of those backing the movement match theirs. Thus, the donors hide their tax loopholes, their financial interests, their pay-to-play schemes, their unsavory associations, their government regulations aimed at gaming the markets, and their money laundering.

Meanwhile, journalists in the mainstream are too busy covering riots and covering for the subversive elements to pay any attention to what happens at these educational nonprofit foundations. These anti-capitalist foundations, their employees, and their benefactors all thrive on civil unrest. They create the chaos that strikes deep divisions between people in American society. And make no mistake—the media thrive on Donald Trump's Twitter account. In today's click-bait news cycle, media outlets nationwide have a financial incentive to pay attention to stories that attract the most consumption. True investigative journalism exposing the bad actors on the Left just doesn't pay.

The media blackout goes even further. All too often, social media giants and national media outlets cooperate with the more activist elements of these nonprofits, granting them inside access and collaborating to decide which stories get reported, and which ones don't. Under the guise of nonpartisan fact-checking, stopping fake news, and efforts at transparency or investigative journalism, several watchdog organizations exist solely to insert a radical progressive tone into the news consumed by millions every night. Some of them are among the most trusted nonpartisan groups in the public opinion business. Too often, the line gets blurred between reflecting results of polls and actively trying to change the results. To put it crudely, this agenda isn't going to advance itself. An ample network of low-profile progressive collaborators, inside and outside the media and Silicon Valley, exists to do just that. The curtain remains drawn, the veil remains unpenetrated, and these forces continue to operate with relative impunity.

This book will penetrate that veil. It will reveal the well-known and not so well-known progressive mega-donors and the agenda they want to implement for America. This book will connect the dots between this progressive agenda and the endless array of nonprofit front groups deployed to implement the agenda. It will reveal the often distasteful relationships many would prefer to remain hidden. It will examine the tricky dealings of the mega-donors and how they made their money in the first place. While a full catalog of all the dirty money would be impossible in such a short passage, it will highlight some of the grimiest relationships as a representation of how rampantly the most subversive of players have taken over our political system. It will shine light on the shady dealings of the front groups, from buying influence with elected officials and exerting pressure on public opinion, to money laundering schemes and shielding their true purpose. This book will also examine whether these dealings are legal, or whether they can reasonably be classified as racketeering. Finally, this book will reveal the true nature of the progressive mega-donor agenda, its not so altruistic goals, and what this agenda means for the future of the United States of America.

This is a look behind the curtain.

CHAPTER 1

DAYS OF RAGE

"In the United States, the working class are Demo-crats. The middle class are Republicans. The upper class are Communists."

—WHITTAKER CHAMBERS

On November 8, 2016, four very different scenes were playing out in separate locations across New York City. That evening, all of America watched public scenes of triumph, heartache, a refusal to face the music, and a quiet, seething anger that quickly turned into an obsession with vengeance. Across the nation, Americans watched New York, and then reacted.

An acutely emotional election year culminated in a shocking ending, with Donald J. Trump's defeat of Hillary Rodham Clinton. The rollicking, unruly, and at times, undisciplined Trump campaign seemed no match for the Clinton machine. To say the results were unexpected is an understatement of vast proportions. The only national poll that had Clinton losing was dismissed as an outlier.[1] Rumors persisted throughout the campaign of Clinton loyalists who had wanted to ensure Trump was the Republican nominee, giving her the best chance at victory. A victory by Trump could not have happened. President Clinton was a foregone conclusion.

For many, the inevitability of Clinton's election made her defeat that much more unbearable. This wasn't merely the sting of tearing off a Band-Aid. For those who were emotionally invested in the outcome of this election, Clinton's defeat was more akin to a Civil War doctor amputating a limb with no anesthetic.

The Jacob K. Javits Convention Center, in the Hell's Kitchen section of Manhattan, is a glitzy, modern conference hall. The Javits Center was chosen for the victory party for America's first woman president, not insignificantly, because of its gleaming glass structures—including a symbolic glass ceiling. This was to be a victory party of historic proportions. As the evening progressed, and as polling results began to emerge, Hillary Clinton supporters turned from jubilation to stunned silence to desolation and tears. Hillary didn't even bother to come out to address her supporters, instead opting to stay in her suite at the Peninsula Hotel on Fifth Avenue, five blocks from Central Park, a long limousine ride from the Javits Center. Sullen, crushed, quarantined from her supporters—that's how Hillary spent that excruciating night.

The image of John Podesta emerging, finally, punishingly late into the night, to tell Hillary supporters at the Javits Center that she would not be addressing them on Election Night put the perfect cap on an astonishing day in American history. It symbolized how out of touch Hillary was with regular Americans. Her supporters were With Her. She was not with them.

Meanwhile, a block and a half away from Hillary's personal hell in her hotel suite, in the New York Hilton Midtown, Donald Trump was also watching history unfold. Far from confident, the Trump team started the evening bracing for the worst. Even the most senior campaign staff members expressed doubt before polls across the nation began closing. One staffer was quoted around seven o'clock saying it would take a miracle to win.[2] By eleven thirty, that miracle had occurred, and the fist-pumping and cocktail drinking had begun. Trump supporters poured in to the ballroom at the Hilton to celebrate. Every news update showing Hillary losing an important state was met with loud cheers. As Hillary shrank from public view in her suite, Trump and his team emerged jubilant and victorious.

The two candidates were physically separated by a mere block and a half, but they might as well have been in different galaxies. Trump addressed the throngs of supporters who came to celebrate, promising, as most presidents-elect do, to unite the nation. Meanwhile, as Hillary wept, her supporters were left to fend for themselves in the cold Manhattan night.

Over in Brooklyn, another scene was unfolding. It resembled the scene at Javits Center. At Clinton Campaign Headquarters, just over the Brooklyn Bridge, the dedicated volunteers slowly came to the realization everything was crumbling around them. For many hours, most of the dedicated operatives in that Brooklyn office building refused to believe what was happening. Counties in Florida hadn't reported! Pennsylvania was too close to call! We can still win without North Carolina! Finally, hope gave way to tears, shock, and awe—but there was also anger. As the reality of a new normal began to set in, that anger became a steeled resolve.

The seething anger began to drive a few select individuals in Hillary's orbit. These men and their patrons had been at the heart of Hillary for President for decades. Despite the evaporation of their visions of glory, they were not the types to fold. They were the types to plot, to play the long game—and to play it dirty. Frenzied phone calls and texts to mega-donors accentuated and intensified the focus of their anger. Disbelief and shock transformed into planning sessions. We simply cannot let this man be successful, they told each other. We need to bring to bear every resource we have at our disposal. We need to come together to probe every weakness, undermine every effort, oppose each and every policy.

We must RESIST.

At the center of this frenzy of communications were two men. These two men were integral to the Clinton machine, and there was no way they were going to let this stunning defeat be the end. One was the longtime Clinton confidante who served as campaign chairman. A government attorney turned political campaign operative and activist, John Podesta is the ultimate DC swamp creature. Podesta's experience in Washington affords him a significant measure of leverage when speaking to elected officials, bureaucrats, and donors. His ability to trade favors and fund public campaigns to advocate for progressive policy gives him enormous sway over the Democratic Party. Podesta founded the Center for American Progress, which boasts an annual budget upwards of $50 million, funded by the biggest players on the Left.[3] He knows where the bodies are buried, as they say. He was the man dispatched to address Hillary's supporters at two o'clock in the morning at the Javits Center after her defeat became inevitable, when Hillary was unable or unwilling to do so herself.

The second man had been a Clinton supporter for more than two decades. No, supporter isn't the right word. This man obsessed over the Clintons throughout his adult life. So much so that he had started out as a vocal—and conservative—critic of both Hillary and President Bill Clinton, before doing a deliberate and public about face and joining their ranks. It's fair to say neither of David Brock's careers would have existed without the Clintons. Brock made his name as a vicious critic of Democrats for conservative periodicals during the Bill Clinton administration. He authored the devastating book *The Real Anita Hill*. Then, after another successful book, he was summoned to write a similar exposé on Hillary Clinton. This book failed to sufficiently savage her, and he lost support on the Right. It was at this point Brock underwent a very public transformation. His endless *mea culpas* included a column in *Esquire* announcing his change of political teams, a memoir, and an open letter to

Bill Clinton (again in *Esquire*) apologizing for his articles that exposed Clinton's corruption and sexual escapades.[4]

That wasn't enough for Brock to grant himself absolution, however. Over the years, Brock has amassed a small army of political nonprofits which take advantage of the tax code to shield donors from scrutiny when possible, and which work to attack conservative viewpoints in the news. Becoming a loyal and steadfast Democratic attack dog has led Brock into the shadowy world of leftist billionaires who prefer to remain behind the scenes—donors who dedicate much of their philanthropy toward efforts to redefine American government. Brock found acceptance among these figures on the Left after he had long ago frittered away his trust on the Right.

Together, Brock and Podesta, both of whom played large roles in creating the image of Hillary's inevitability, thought their work had culminated in another President Clinton. Instead, upon the realization they would have to face a world in which Donald Trump served as president, they found themselves picking up the pieces and attempting to rally the resistance. The election results were still unfolding as the two political veterans realized what was happening, and what needed to be done next.

You see, there would be no loyal opposition. There would be no attempting to work with this president. He would not be given a chance to succeed. There simply could not be any tolerance, any peaceful coexistence, despite their bumper stickers to the contrary. There would only be resistance. Indeed, this process started during the campaign, when they brought public pressure to bear on their friends and allies in the mainstream media. Trump could not be allowed to be normalized or accepted.

The political operatives and their mega-donors knew an opportunity when they saw one.

Brock attended some election return watch parties but left early as things deteriorated. As Trump supporters began to party at the Hilton Midtown, Brock was on his way to visit some important patrons.[5] An unseasonably warm day had turned into a chilly night, but Brock was probably too consumed by thought to notice. He visited with George Soros. He called other donors. Eventually he ended up on the roof of a high rise, overlooking the East River, just up the street from the Arthur M. Sackler Foundation building on Sutton Place.[6] He commiserated with another longtime Clinton operative, James Carville, over the phone, and began to form the seeds of a plan. He fired off a memo to his longtime friend and in-house fundraiser, Mary Pat Bonner.[7] He spoke with more donors deep into the early morning before finally going to bed.

———

The next night, riots broke out across the United States.[8] A relatively unknown group called Antifa, along with several affiliated groups, ramped up quickly to organize many of them in cities on the East and West Coasts. The riots lasted the better part of a week, and the organizers made no effort to curtail the violence.[9] Indeed, what passes for leadership in these loosely organized groups tacitly—and often explicitly—encouraged the violence.

They were aided by big-city mayors and city councils that sympathized with them, looked the other way, and in many cases ordered the police to stand down.[10] Large mobs took over streets, closed down freeways, caused millions in property damage, and terrorized countless residents in major metropolitan areas.[11]

Made up of several different factions, Antifa took its name from the militant pro-communist group opposing the Nazi Party in 1930s Germany—Antifaschistische Aktion.[12] They grew out of the writings of Marx and Engels and the spirit of revolution. As the Bolsheviks had done in Russia, they wanted to bring revolution and collectivism to Germany. Their sworn enemy was the rising Nazi Party, fascists that opposed every form of communism. Antifaschistische Aktion took pride in bringing the fight to the fascists in the streets.

Antifa in America takes its justification for existence from Antifaschistische Aktion, and looks nostalgically upon their street brawls with German fascists. Antifa hopes to bring a widespread revolution against capitalism to America. They formed with members from previous movements like the anarchists at the World Trade Organization riots in Seattle in 1999, Occupy Wall Street, and several other radical groups which have waged violent protests over the years. Their stated purpose is to take "direct action" to oppose anyone they determine to be a modern-day fascist.[13] This direct action does not mean peaceable assembly. Direct action means proactively blocking speakers they don't like, setting things on fire, opposing the police at every turn, forming large mobs to block traffic, and preparing for violent confrontations. In many riots on the West

Coast, the Antifa mobs gathered crude weapons like bricks, pipes, and bags of human urine and feces to hurl at their targets.[14] They also infiltrated other demonstrations which were intended to include a peaceful march, with the deliberate purpose of turning nonviolent protests into violent confrontations with seemingly anyone who got in their way.[15] As the months passed in 2017, Antifa subsequently targeted pro-Trump rallies, speaking engagements by prominent conservatives, and even mundane activities of local Republican Party organizations, with predictable results.[16]

To casual observers, it appeared Antifa formed overnight and began a reign of terror in America's streets. The truth is much deeper than that.

———

Over the winter, as the calendar flipped from 2016 to 2017, liberals all over America fretted. How could they #resist? How could they stop this horrible man? How could they prove he colluded with the Russians to steal the election? How soon after his inauguration could he be impeached? They quickly formed the Women's March, drawing a few hundred thousand protesters to the National Mall the day after Inauguration Day. Local marches occurred across the nation as well.

These marches started as raw reactions on social media to the election of President Trump. Soon, however, some of the best-funded organizations of the institutional Left in America took them over and co-opted them for their own purposes.

In December 2016, Indivisible appeared. An article for KQED, a public broadcasting outlet in Northern California, led with the headline: "Who's Funding the Anti-Trump Movement? We Don't Know." It was a first look at Indivisible, and the Indivisible Guide. Activists not so prone to violence, who wanted to protect the progressive legacy of President Obama, geared up to create a protest network modeled on the success of the American Tea Party Movement. They framed the open question of funding as a shadowy secret. Of course, had the KQED reporters bothered looking on the Indivisible website, it would have become immediately obvious who was behind this new movement.[17, 18]

———

A week after the 2016 election, a group of the biggest donors on the Left met in Washington, DC for a semi-annual planning session. The Democracy Alliance (DA), first formed in 2005 in the wake of Democrat John Kerry's failed attempt to win the presidency back from the incumbent Republican, George W. Bush. Co-founded by George Soros, the DA insists on secrecy, preferring to shield its members from public scrutiny.[19] The agenda for the November 2017 meeting states this explicitly: "DA conference participants are entitled to the expectation that their conference experience and their identity should remain confidential. In order to keep faith with that expectation, we ask Partners and guests to:

- Respect the privacy of others and not share Partners' names or details of the conference with the press or post to personal media channels including, but not limited to, Facebook, Twitter, Instagram, YouTube, etc.

- Contact Elizabeth Bartolomeo at ebartolomeo@democracyalliance.org or (202) 255-2677 if you are contacted by the media or a blogger about the conference.

- Refrain from leaving sensitive materials out where others may find them. We ask that all attendees dispose of unwanted conference materials in specially-identified recycling bins.

Of course, the DA also intended the agenda to remain private, but the conservative news outlet Washington Free Beacon sent a couple of reporters and foiled those plans.[20] Since their formation, the DA has met twice a year to strategically plan their funding of progressive nonprofit groups across the country. DA boasts about 120 active members. In order to become a member, partners must commit to making at least $200,000 per year in donations to DA-approved organizations. These approved organizations include goals such as battling climate change, strengthening public sector unions, repealing *Citizens United*, fighting for the $15 minimum wage, and other leftist ideals. The Winter Meeting in 2016, directly following Election Day, originally planned to strategize and push President Clinton further to the left. Instead, the DA quickly retooled the agenda and plotted ways to fund the resistance to President Trump. In fact, after Election Day, DA added a moderated discussion with none other than George Soros to the agenda.[21]

This was not the only effort to bring mega-donors and well-heeled activists on the Left together to direct their considerable resources in opposition to the new president and his agenda. There would be many more such meetings throughout 2017. Their goal: discrediting conservatives throughout American life and sowing the seeds of division across society. The politics of personal destruction would play a prominent role in all of these new strategies, in defense of the progressive agenda advanced under President Obama.

———

Two and a half months after Election Day, as Donald Trump was being sworn in as America's forty-fifth president, David Brock was hosting another conference to lay out his plan. Deliberately timed for Inauguration Weekend, this conference punctuated the pain of living in an America with Donald Trump as president. The conference was Brock's attempt to consolidate players in the movement: activists, Democratic Party leaders, nonprofit organizations, and most importantly, money. Of course, this consolidation would revolve around Brock's own organizations. The biggest names in left-leaning politics gathered to commiserate and to plan. Brock sent a straightforward appeal email to potential attendees: "What better way to spend inaugural weekend than talking about how to kick Donald Trump's ass?"[22]

As luck would have it, the Washington Free Beacon caught wind of this conference as well and sent two undercover reporters to witness the event. They got their hands on Brock's self-congratulatory and self-promoting blueprint.[23] The plan is as bold as it is outrageous. It calls for a constellation of leftist organizations to unite in common cause to target conservatives for destruction.

Many of those organizations and the billionaires who run them were at the conference that weekend. So, too, were all the candidates running to replace the deposed Debbie Wasserman Schultz as chair of the Democratic National Committee, as well as seasoned Democratic attack dogs masquerading as journalists such as Keith Olbermann. They joked with one another about how much they drank on Election Night. They railed against the conservative efforts to repeal the progressive agenda they helped to put in place over the previous eight years. They talked about how they could undermine the new administration at every turn.

The irony of such a conference, and such a network of billionaire funders, runs deep. The popular narrative of progressives goes like this: they back the little guy, they oppose Wall Street bankers, they promote tolerance and value diversity, and their policies favor the middle class and not rich fat cats. They make the claim that uneducated white voters, when they vote Republican, vote against their own self-interest. Bernie Sanders refused to form a super PAC (political action committee) to support his campaign, and railed against political donations from billionaires. He bragged the average donation to his campaign

was $40. Repealing the *Citizens United* decision with a consti-
tutional amendment became a *cause célèbre*, despite most folks
not understanding what it meant.

The reality of the progressive movement differs greatly
from this grassroots narrative. The DNC candidates were
summoned to perform for their billionaire benefactors and
judged on their worthiness to run the party. The candidates
competed to out-flank one another to the left, appealing to the
Obama-inspired progressivism which has come to define the
Democratic Party itself.

Crafting the future of the DNC was only one small part
of the conference. A much larger resistance effort was being
formed. In the introduction to the blueprint, Brock writes:

> "We have the mandate. Together, we won the popular vote
> and Democrats picked up seats in the Senate and in the
> House. Trump is the least popular incoming president in
> modern history and the outgoing president and popular
> vote winner are again the most admired man and woman
> in the nation. The country did not vote for Trump-style
> change. Trump has the legal authority, but we have the moral
> authority—and the moral responsibility—to oppose him. We
> will fight every day." He goes on to say they will resist the
> normalization of Donald Trump.[24]

Sounds familiar, doesn't it? It's almost as if Brock has been
writing the headlines blaring across the mainstream media
since Election Day.

Indeed, Brock implemented this plan well before the election. Using his foundation, Media Matters for America, Brock

and crew proactively contact media outlets all over the country. Presenting themselves as a nonpartisan and nonprofit enterprise, they offer to help media members to avoid pro-conservative bias in their reporting. Typically, they find all too friendly reporters to take their calls. The Blueprint (or, if you prefer, the Plan to Kick Trump's Ass) lays out the tactics in extensive, self-congratulatory detail.

It doesn't stop there. In the Blueprint, Brock brags about having direct access to the raw data from Twitter and Facebook.[25] He writes:

> "Media monitoring enables us to identify pernicious misinformation and develop strategies for combating it. Historically, this has meant monitoring conservative media, television news, and newspapers.
>
> "But relying on human media monitors is no longer sustainable. Fake news and alt-right communities are multiplying exponentially.
>
> *"Media Matters has already secured access to raw data from Facebook, Twitter, and other social media sites...[w]e will now develop technologies and processes to systematically monitor and analyze this unfiltered data." (emphasis added)*

Of course, Facebook, Twitter, and the other major social media outlets have no obligation to take recommendations from Media Matters to alter their algorithms. Then again, when the CEOs and many of the members of the boards of directors of Facebook, Twitter, Google, Amazon, Wikipedia, LinkedIn, and many other tech giants in Silicon Valley lean left themselves, such a partnership doesn't seem so far-fetched.

Besides, we've seen this effort work in the past. Media Matters successfully got itself inserted into the Girl Scouts of America in 2010 as a "nonpartisan watchdog" that school-age girls could use as a resource to determine the truthfulness of a given news story. A workbook called "MEdia" aimed to help young girls avoid passing around rumors, innuendos, and urban legends online. Somehow, Media Matters for America—which does not attempt to shield its anti-conservative bias—made the list of trusted online fact-checking sources. As of 2015, the Girl Scouts had new editions of the workbook still in circulation for their members.[26] Brock and Media Matters have a long history of worming their way into public discourse, with the goal of shifting it leftward.

Indeed, the galaxy of groups founded by and run by Brock all claim the simultaneous goals of fighting bias in the news and undermining conservative discourse, often litigating to get the results they want.[27] This contradiction doesn't seem to faze David Brock, who founded, runs, or advises more than a dozen such nonprofits and super PACs. In fact, fourteen of them are housed in the same office suite in Washington, often sharing employees, paying rent to one another, making grants back and forth among themselves, and fundraising from the same sources.[28]

So what did Brock's Plan to Kick Trump's Ass actually entail? The plan contains four parts, each to be undertaken by a Brock entity. Again, thanks to the Washington Free Beacon, we have the actual printed plan, which includes:

Media Matters for America

In the next four years, Media Matters will continue its core mission of disarming right-wing misinformation, while leading the fight against the next generation of conservative disinformation: The proliferation of fake news and propaganda now threatening the country's information ecosystem. Here's what success will look like:

- Serial misinformers and right-wing propagandists inhabiting everything from social media to the highest levels of government will be exposed, discredited.

- Internet and social media platforms, like Google and Facebook, will no longer uncritically and without consequence host and enrich fake news sites and propagandists.

- Toxic alt-right social media-fueled harassment campaigns that silence dissent and poison our national discourse will be punished and halted.

American Bridge 21st Century PAC

American Bridge will cement itself as the standard-bearer of opposition research, build on its role as a progressive clearinghouse for information that drives the narrative on Republican officeholders and candidates, and be at the epicenter of Democrats' work to regain power—starting in 2017 and building to 2020. Here's what success will look like:

- Trump will be defeated either through impeachment or at the ballot box in 2020.

- The balance of power will shift back to Democrats. We will measurably impact US Senate, gubernatorial, and state legislative races.

- We will free ourselves from solely relying on the press. Our robust digital program will reach voters directly online.

Citizens for Responsibility and Ethics in Washington (CREW)

CREW will be the leading nonpartisan ethics watchdog group in a period of crisis with a president and administration that present possible conflicts of interest and ethical problems on an unprecedented scale. CREW will demand ethical conduct from the administration and all parts of government, expose improper influence from powerful interest, and ensure accountability when the administration and others shirk ethical standards, rules, and laws. Here's what success will look like:

- Trump will be afflicted by a steady flow of damaging information, new revelations, and an inability to avoid conflicts issues.

- The Trump administration will be forced to defend illegal conduct in court.

- Powerful industries and interest groups will see their influence wane.

- Dark money will be a political liability in key states.

ShareBlue

ShareBlue will take back social media for Democrats. We will delegitimize Donald Trump's presidency by emboldening the opposition and empowering the majority of Americans who oppose him. Shareblue will be the dynamic nucleus of a multi-platform media company that informs, engages, and arms Americans to fight. Here's what success will look like:

- Shareblue will become the de facto news outlet for opposition leaders and the grassroots.

- Trump allies will be forced to step down or change course due to news pushed by Shareblue.

- Under pressure from Shareblue, Democrats will take more aggressive positions against Trump.

- Shareblue will achieve financial sustainability while diversifying content offerings and platforms.

- Top editorial and writing talent will leave competitors to join Shareblue.[29]

Between his charity organizations, educational foundations, super PACs, hybrid PACs, and all of his nonprofit entities, Brock has weaponized his assets while taking advantage of

Internal Revenue Service codes affording him tax-exempt status, and affording his donors a large measure of anonymity.

All of these groups on the Left, funded by semiannual Democracy Alliance meetings, the Environmental Grantmakers Association, the series of Brock's Democracy Matters conferences, Soros and Steyer, Sussman and Gates, Stein and Sandler, Buffett and Sackler, Hewlett and Packard, Rockefeller and Ford and Pew, and all the other mega-donors in the progressive universe, derive their moral justification from an array of nonprofits, think tanks, and thought leaders on the Left. They fund such groups as ProPublica, Pew Charitable Trusts, the Southern Poverty Law Center, the Union of Concerned Scientists, and other nonprofits that grant progressive causes the intellectual coverage they need to justify their campaigns. In turn, these organizations provide grants to an even wider network of groups which advance the agenda of progressivism in the mainstream consciousness. Grants flow back and forth within this web of organizations, shielding donors from blame for the actions of this outlet or that. Meanwhile, they produce work under the guise of nonpartisanship that makes its way into the public consciousness, with news consumers mostly unaware they contribute to the mainstreaming of radical leftist ideology.

Take the Pew Charitable Trusts, for instance. Most Americans know a particular Pew brand: a fairly reliable public opinion polling organization with no apparent bias.[30] Media outlets across the country use their public opinion research and constantly cite the nonpartisan nature of the organization. Through their nonprofit 501(c)(3) charity, Pew Research

Center, they conduct research often cited by the mainstream media. According to their website, "Pew Research Center is a nonprofit, tax-exempt 501(c)3 organization and a subsidiary of The Pew Charitable Trusts, our primary funder. The Center's empirically driven research on a wide range of topics helps key stakeholders in society—policymakers, media and the public at large—understand and solve the world's most challenging problems. As a neutral source of data and analysis, Pew Research Center does not take policy positions."[31] This makes up the public face of Pew for the vast majority of Americans who don't examine what the larger organization does. Pew Research is a smaller affiliate, and grantee, of a much larger organization, Pew Charitable Trusts (PCT).

PCT has its tentacles in lots and lots of leftist causes. With almost a billion dollars in net assets, according to their 2015 IRS Form 990, PCT's grantmaking reaches much further than many realize. That year, they reported $710,716,507 in total revenue, $118,756,786 in salaries paid, and $110,599,511 in grants awarded. This sizeable grantmaking operation funded all manners of highly partisan efforts. According to Capital Research Center (CRC), for almost two decades, PCT has funded efforts to severely limit the First Amendment through campaign finance reform and net neutrality. Scott Walter, president of CRC, reported in 2011, "The Pew Charitable Trusts and a small group of left-of-center grantmakers have launched repeated crusades to control Americans' speech, whether it's expressed in political campaigns, newspapers, or television and radio. Their latest effort aims to bring speech over the internet to heel. But even some left-wingers suspect the goal is not to help the average citizen but to defend elite gatekeepers' control over the nation's conversations."[32] With the assets they control, their grantmaking ability affords them a measure of clout in the public discourse possessed by few other organizations.

Of course, much like the progressive movement as a whole, this enormous partisan operation runs counter to the public perception of the Pew brand. A deliberate and meticulous effort has put a public face on Pew that creates the perception of a nonpartisan charity.

Members of the progressive movement want it that way. In an all too common theme on the professional Left, the public perception belies the true goals. Just like the Democracy Alliance playbook, David Brock's Blueprint promises donor confidentiality and exhorts attendees to keep all distributed materials away from prying eyes. The Democracy Matters conference only issued press credentials for the opening remarks and for a very select few events.

They must have good reasons to conceal their identities and their agenda. The tax-exempt organizations to which they donate certainly have the opportunity to avoid disclosing their benefactors, especially as they pass money from charitable organizations to more overtly political organizations.

Why do they conceal their identities and their real agenda?

CHAPTER 2

TIDE POD FINANCING

"When plunder becomes a way of life for a group of men in a society, over the course of time they create for themselves a legal system that authorizes it and a moral code that glorifies it."

—Frédéric Bastiat

In October 2017, an up-and-coming reporter obsessed with numbers did something which escaped notice by most of America. Indeed, the practice he uncovered is so arcane and yet so widespread, many may not recognize it as shady. The implications of this reporter's action could lead to devastating consequences for progressive nonprofits, although he says that was not his intent. Absent his singular obsession with making numbers match across reports, the discrepancies which look a lot like money laundering may never have been uncovered.

Andrew Kerr is a self-described computer geek. As a new college grad a few years back, Kerr quickly found success as a technical account manager for Microsoft. Well compensated at a young age, and long before thinking about getting married and settling down, Kerr decided on a course correction. He had never gotten much involved in politics until the run-up to the 2016 presidential cycle, when he realized this election would significantly affect his future. Looking around, like many other voters, he saw manipulations and spin and fake news shaping the way voters perceived the two presidential candidates. So when he discovered some, shall we say, reporting irregularities in the finances of Media Matters for America, he decided to dig in.

Kerr graciously agreed to explain his investigation for this book. "I was a computer geek growing up—I mean, I worked for Geek Squad during college, about as nerdy as you can get," Kerr said in an extensive interview. "Then I got a really nice job at Microsoft as a technical account manager. It kind of clicked for me in about mid-summer 2016. The presidential election was really heating up. Then I kind of cultivated this passion for journalism. I have a background in technology, but I've always been passionate about US public policy. So my experience in the business world, combining all three of those, I'm able to look at Media Matters' tax return documents and see things that are plain as day to me, that have been out there for years, but that nobody has been reporting on yet."

Those tax forms, the IRS Form 990, contain a wealth of information for anyone with the patience and persistence to look. As a newcomer to journalism and politics, Kerr didn't quite know where to turn, but he knew he had a big story on his hands. He also knew he didn't want to be pigeon-holed as a Republican shill. "I think that there's a lot of need in journalism just for solid reporting on the facts. I am being honest about that. That is my primary concern, that they are breaking the rules. It's not that I went after them because they're liberal and I'm conservative. It's just because they're doing a bad thing, and the right thing to do was to call them out."

His efforts to remain nonpartisan have not escaped the notice of voters on the Left. Kerr says, "Even though we're calling out partisan organizations, it doesn't need to be partisan. One of the coolest things about this experience was getting emails from Bernie Sanders supporters. It's no secret that Bernie Sanders got really screwed over. I've gotten a number of emails from people on the left. All this talk about election integrity, the base of that argument is correct. We need to have honest elections in this country. A level playing field. If these organizations are breaking the rules and benefiting from it, that's just not fair. It's not right."

And call them out, he did, in the form of a complaint to the Federal Election Commission in October 2017.[1] That didn't occur, however, until after months of research, review with attorneys, and poring over the numbers with numerous forensic accountants. Of the complaint, Kerr says, "I was just a concerned citizen. A lot of people got looped up into the 2016 elections for a lot of different reasons. I was honestly just curious about how our system works—super PAC and political action committees, political nonprofits, dark money, that's all really confusing. So I was just curious and wanted to learn more. I looked at Media Matters for America as an example. I was just going to look through their tax return documents and try to learn through that as an example. I intentionally chose Media Matters because they're in the news a lot, they have a great level of influence. It didn't take long before I started noticing the money transfers from Media Matters to all their organizations, and started noticing all the shared office space and The Bonner Group. I really quickly realized nobody is talking about this. I don't think this would have come out if I didn't say anything."

Of course, The Bonner Group refers to Brock's in-house fundraising contractor, run by Mary Pat Bonner. Even *The New York Times* has caught wind of her, noting in a front-page report in February 2015 that Brock and Bonner share a summer rental in the Hamptons.[2] That report went into some detail over other possible lapses in ethics, including her commission structure for fundraising.

So, what did Kerr discover? He spells it out as a three-layered problem. The complexity of this multi-layered problem required an extensive "explainer" piece at his blog, TheCitizensAudit.com.[3] Notably, the complexity of these potential reporting violations creates convenient cover for David Brock, Mary Pat Bonner, American 21st Century Bridge PAC, Media Matters for America, The Franklin Forum, ShareBlue, CREW, Correct the Record, and the other orbiting bodies in the galaxy of nonprofits run by Brock and crew. The difficulty in matching IRS reports, FEC reports, and required financial reports to corporation divisions in individual states allows all sorts of malfeasance to escape notice by all but the most fastidious of observers.

Kerr says he deliberately chose the Federal Election Commission for the formal complaint, over the IRS, because the FEC is required by law to respond to any complaint. "There have been many complaints filed on Media Matters to the IRS," says Kerr. "The argument was that Media Matters was set up as an educational organization, but their content is clearly partisan, they should be labeled as a political organization, they should lose their charitable status."

Good luck getting a response, says Kerr. "The IRS is not required to respond to it. They're not even required to acknowledge that they received it. They have no time frame to issue any sort of ruling."

Given the acknowledged shenanigans the IRS pulled in choosing not to grant tax exempt status to Tea Party and conservative groups, there remains little doubt the IRS has been used as a weapon against political opponents in a staggering variety of ways. In fact, the conservative voter integrity group True The Vote, of Houston, Texas, sued the IRS over the scrutiny they received when applying for nonprofit status. The judge in the case issued a consent decree in January 2018 in which the IRS admitted to all of their biased targeting over the years.[4]

The FEC has a reputation for being mere political theater.[5] Despite this, the statutes governing the agency actually require several positive actions to be taken. They must acknowledge and respond to the complaint within sixty days, and they must hold a vote on whether or not to investigate the complaint. Ironically, another Brock nonprofit, Citizens for Responsibility and Ethics in Washington (CREW), uses the FEC for just this purpose when trying to take down their targets. "CREW frequently files litigation against the FEC," says Kerr. "CREW files a lot of FEC complaints, and when FEC doesn't do what they want them to do, they take legal action against the FEC. The reason why I'm saying this, unlike the IRS, with the FEC, there's a structure. The FEC is required to take in the complaint. They're required to do these things in this time frame. The public has a right to know the results of the investigation. Unlike the IRS, where you throw it into a black hole and cross your fingers that maybe they'll look at it in the next decade or so."

In order to understand Kerr's FEC complaint, one must understand the difference between a 501(c)(3), a 501(c)(4), a 527, a super PAC, and all the other different types of IRS-defined nonprofits that may or may not engage in some sort of political activity. Depending on the type of entity, and how funds get passed back and forth between them, there may be grounds to charge those funds are being improperly used for restricted activities under IRS and FEC regulations.

The IRS defines a 501(c)(3) as a nonprofit organization involved in charity. Most political 501(c)(3) organizations are designated as educational foundations. They exist to educate the public on a particular issue or set of issues. Donations to a 501(c)(3) are tax-deductible. Donors are not required to be disclosed on IRS filing forms (Form 990). This is an important distinction, because donations to other types of organizations must be disclosed. Lobbying, candidate work, political advocacy, and the like must not make up a substantial portion of the organization's activities. Generally that's taken to mean less than 10 percent to 20 percent of the work done by the organization.

A 501(c)(4) falls into one of two categories: a social welfare organization, or an association of local employees. These organizations can engage in lobbying and advocacy efforts, as long as those don't exceed 50 percent of their organizational purpose. 501(c)(4)s also don't have to disclose their donors to the IRS on their 990s, but donations are not tax deductible like they are to a 501(c)(3).

527s are political organizations and committees, and include political parties as well as PACs and super PACs. These organizations must report all financial transactions to the FEC and cannot shield donors. Donations do not qualify for tax-exempt status. They typically support issues, public policy, or candidates. Candidates set up PACs to support their campaigns. Donations from individuals to candidates cannot exceed $2,700 per election cycle. super PACs exist as a result of the ruling in the *Citizens United* case, which said independent organizations cannot be held to any expenditure limits, so long as messages and expenditures are independent and not coordinated with a candidate or campaign.

The first of the three layers of Kerr's FEC complaint against Media Matters relates to the common paymaster arrangement employed by many nonprofits to save on expenses. Kerr noticed the tax forms for American Bridge 21st Century PAC, Franklin

Forum, Correct the Record, and several others included rent payments to Media Matters for America. These organizations all share office space, employees, and in several cases, even a main phone number. According to Kerr, who reviewed the IRS Form 990s for all these organizations, "David Brock has 7 non-profits, 3 super PACs, one 527-committee, one LLC, one joint fundraising committee, and one unregistered solicitor crammed into his office in Washington DC."

Right off the bat, this appears...well...off. How could so many supposedly separate nonprofit organizations share a common paymaster and all occupy the same office when at least some of them are not supposed to be coordinating efforts? How could entities that share employees owe rent to one another? How could all of these entities utilize the same professional solicitor—an in-house fundraising contractor? And why isn't the professional solicitor properly registered?

Now, the District of Columbia does not require individual fundraisers to register, but it does require fundraising firms to register. We will examine this distinction later on in this chapter. For now, let's let The Bonner Group explain for themselves who they are as an entity: "The Bonner Group is a Washington, D.C.-based progressive nonprofit and Democratic political fundraising firm. Our clients include some of the most prominent and effective progressive organizations across the country. Over the past 18 years, the Bonner Group has worked for major nonprofit organizations, Presidential campaigns, House & Senate campaigns, Gubernatorial campaigns, ballot initiatives, capital campaigns and '527' organizations."[6]

The arrangement with The Bonner Group caused Brock some serious heartburn among his patrons after the *New York Times* article in February 2015. Many of the donors, organizers, and players in the Democracy Alliance took exception to this arrangement, sharing their fears they would need to deal exclusively with Bonner to maintain the same level of access and influence they had previously wielded.[7] When Bonner moved her entire operation into Brock's offices in 2014, it only exacerbated this discomfort. Several donors publicly questioned whether it was ethical for Bonner to take her standard 12.5 percent commission on all donations received—a practice the industry group Association of Fundraising Professionals considers counter to its code of ethical standards.[8] As we'll see later in this chapter, a commission-based fundraising contract is the least of the ethical concerns raised by this relationship between Bonner and Brock.

But first, back to the first underlying layer of Kerr's FEC complaint—the in-house, unregistered solicitor. On their IRS forms, and in states where The Bonner Group Inc. bothered to register as a business with the Secretaries of State, they list their main place of business as 455 Massachusetts Avenue, NW, Suite 640—the same business address as Media Matters, 21stCentury American Bridge, Franklin Forum, and all the other Brock entities.[9] Thirty nine states and the District of Columbia require a professional fundraiser to register for a solicitation license with the Secretary of State (or the Department of Regulatory Affairs in DC). At the time Kerr began digging into Media Matters prior to the 2016 election, The Bonner Group showed up on the DC corporation registry—but their license to do business in DC had been revoked. It remains in this status as of this writing.[10] Not only that, The Bonner Group never registered for a professional solicitation license required by the Department of Regulatory Affairs in DC.[11]

That's just the DC registry. In other states where The Bonner Group operates, Kerr went poking around and found similar registration issues. Their registration lapsed years ago in Florida. They claim to do business in Illinois but have never registered there. The same goes for Maryland. However, their registration in Massachusetts is up to date, and they seem to file regular reports as required with the Attorney General's office. Not so in New Jersey, however—no registration exists there. At least they tried in Virginia, but the registration is still pending after several years.[12]

Look, filling out paperwork and filing it with state after state after state is tedious. It's boring. And it can be expensive if you hire professional staff to do it. The consequences of blowing it off, however, can cost your organization. Should any of these states choose to investigate, The Bonner Group could be liable for hefty fines, or could be forced out of business altogether in the state.

Safe to say, The Bonner Group has a pretty well-established pattern of playing fast and loose with the rules on the state reporting level. That attitude appears to carry over to how they conduct their federal reporting, and who gets to pay their contingency fees. Remember, they share office space in the Brock galaxy housed on the sixth floor of 455 Mass Ave. NW. As Kerr points out, they also receive a commission—usually, but not always, 12.5 percent—on any money passed around from PAC to foundation to charity to super PAC.[13]

That's right, Kerr's investigation reveals The Bonner Group charges a commission on donations or grants awarded from one nonprofit to another. This is money already given by a donor, and presumably already charged a commission when the original donation arrived. Further investigation should be undertaken to determine the extent to which The Bonner Group double dips on its charged commissions.

Now, why would one nonprofit award a grant to another nonprofit which happens to sit in the same office or just down the hall? Especially given the restrictions on political activity for charities, and restrictions on coordinated fundraising and messaging for political committees?

This gets back to what Kerr describes as the first layer of his FEC complaint. On the surface, it seems like a violation for some of these different types of groups to share expenses, employees, and office space. Several such entities can use a common paymaster, however, under a cost-sharing agreement. In filing for tax-exempt status as a 501(c)(4) in 2013, American Bridge 21st Century Foundation (AB Foundation) filled out IRS Form 1024. On this application, AB Foundation described the cost sharing agreement they entered with AB Super PAC:[14]

"The Foundation shares some resources, facilities, and employees with American Bridge 21st Century, a section 527 organization registered with, and reporting to, the Federal Election Commission. The two entities have entered into a cost-sharing agreement to allocate shared costs so neither entity is financially supporting the activities of the other. The two organizations share one overlapping director, David Brock, and they have overlapping officers."

Later in the application, they clearly state they will use employee time sheets to differentiate activities performed for the Foundation versus those performed for the super PAC:

"The organization tracks its expenses, including through the use of timesheets for its employees, to ensure political activities do not become a majority of its activities in the course of a fiscal year, and to ensure that all required taxes will be paid under Internal Revenue Code section 527(f)."[15]

So, while such a cost-sharing agreement doesn't violate any campaign finance or reporting laws, it requires strict account-ing and record keeping to ensure when money gets transferred from the Foundation to the super PAC, it applies to a legally allowed function and accurately reflects the actual time spent by the employees or value of the shared expenses. In the case of AB Foundation, they send money regularly to AB Super PAC as reimbursement for shared expenses. The (c)(4) Foundation lists no employees and does not issue W-2 forms. Instead, they reimburse the super PAC for shared employee expenses, with the work of the Foundation presumably done by super PAC employees.

According to Kerr's analysis of tax forms, those reimburse-ments from the Foundation to the super PAC range into the millions of dollars. During the period of 2011 through the first part of 2017, AB Foundation paid AB Super PAC a total of

$11,116,209.08 in shared expense reimbursements. In a comprehensive, step-wise analysis, Kerr found several red flags in the reporting from both AB Foundation and AB Super PAC. Kerr says, "It didn't take very long at all to notice that money is being passed from one place to another, and nobody's reporting on it. So when I saw these money transfers and the doubling up on the commission, I was like, Okay, what are other people saying about this? Is this legal? What's the explanation? Nobody's talking about it. It blew my mind. I'm sitting on this explosive story, right in the middle of the most contentious election in modern times, with these organizations that are very clearly influencing public opinion during the election, and nobody's talking about this."

The first red flag pops up when comparing the yearly reimbursement amounts from the Foundation to the super PAC. The first sixteen months under this common-paymaster agreement, AB Foundation paid the super PAC a total of $594,823 for reimbursement of employee compensation. During the same period, they paid $86,277 in rent. The amounts of employee reimbursement sharply increase over the next several years, while the rent payments remain relatively flat. By 2015, employee compensation payments jumped to $2,274,352 for the year, while they paid $93,057 in rent.

Kerr runs through several possible explanations of this:

1. It becomes increasingly more cramped in AB Foundation's portion of the office as the years go by. (UNLIKELY)

2. AB Super PAC is financially supporting AB Foundation by footing a larger portion of its occupancy and office expenses each passing year.

3. This would mean AB Foundation wasn't being truthful to the IRS in claiming its cost-sharing agreement ensured neither entity financially supported the activities of the other.

4. AB Foundation's reported employee compensation expenditures are not honest.[16]

Several organizations have asked American Bridge 21st Century to clarify these discrepancies, and every time they have refused comment. For instance, the Sunlight Foundation describes itself as "a national, nonpartisan, nonprofit organization that uses civic technologies, open data, policy analysis, and journalism to make our government and politics more accountable and transparent to all."[17] In a report on February 10, 2016, they detailed several transfers made between related PACs and organizations run by Brock.[18] They reached out to American Bridge for comment but received no response. This pattern repeats itself every time Brock and his organizations receive such specific questions.

The second red flag is in the amounts themselves. Kerr examined the payments made by the Foundation to the super PAC between 2011 and 2015. At first, the payments appear above board:[19]

Contributor	Date	Amount	Purpose
AB Foundation	5/23/2011	$15,796.18	Overhead and Staff Expenses
AB Foundation	6/23/2011	$6,944.46	Overhead and Staff Expenses
AB Foundation	8/4/2011	$6,944.46	Overhead and Staff Expenses
AB Foundation	8/30/2011	$4,306.00	Overhead and Staff Expenses
AB Foundation	8/30/2011	$24,154.29	Overhead Expenses
AB Foundation	8/30/2011	$15,207.98	Overhead Expenses
AB Foundation	8/30/2011	$10,174.95	Overhead and Staff Expenses
AB Foundation	9/22/2011	$32,496.83	Overhead and Staff Expenses
AB Foundation	10/19/2011	$34,093.63	Overhead and Staff Expenses
AB Foundation	10/27/2011	$33,295.23	Overhead and Staff Expenses
AB Foundation	11/28/2011	$42,194.30	Overhead and Staff Expenses
AB Foundation	12/30/2011	$20,058.78	Overhead and Staff Expenses
AB Foundation	2/23/2012	$89,566.67	Overhead and Staff Expenses
AB Foundation	6/15/2012	$234,575.50	Overhead and Staff Expenses
AB Foundation	9/27/2012	$336,087.91	Overhead and Staff Expenses
AB Foundation	11/15/2012	$140,293.33	Overhead and Staff Expenses
AB Foundation	2/7/2013	$247,788.75	Overhead and Staff Expenses
AB Foundation	4/11/2013	$134,200.66	Overhead and Staff Expenses
AB Foundation	5/27/13	$175,490.27	Overhead and Staff Expenses

Note the payments are for specific amounts, which makes sense given that Kerr previously demonstrated that over 90 percent of the payments from the Foundation to the super PAC were for shared employee costs. One would expect the payments to vary in amount based on the number of hours worked on various Foundation projects by super PAC employees.

Payments started to change, however, beginning in 2014:[20]

Contributor	Date	Amount	Purpose
AB Foundation	7/19/2013	$98,122.73	
AB Foundation	7/19/2013	$26,877.27	Overhead and Staff Expenses
AB Foundation	11/13/2013	$321,528.61	Overhead and Staff Expenses
AB Foundation	12/13/2013	$100,678.84	Overhead and Staff Expenses
AB Foundation	1/23/2014	$109,027.93	
AB Foundation	1/31/2014	$27,637.73	
AB Foundation	4/4/2014	$50,000.00	Overhead and Staff Expenses
AB Foundation	4/11/2014	$100,000.00	Overhead and Staff Expenses
AB Foundation	5/19/2014	$50,000.00	Overhead and Staff Expenses
AB Foundation	5/28/2014	$195,364.86	
AB Foundation	5/28/2014	$371,938.22	
AB Foundation	6/27/2014	$99,245.09	Overhead and Staff Expenses
AB Foundation	9/30/2014	$100,000.00	Overhead and Staff Expenses
AB Foundation	10/10/2014	$83,002.47	Overhead and Staff Expenses
AB Foundation	10/10/2014	$400,000.00	Overhead and Staff Expenses
AB Foundation	11/6/2014	$192,728.95	
AB Foundation	11/13/2014	$200,000.00	Overhead and Staff Expenses
AB Foundation	12/19/2014	$167,000.00	Overhead and Staff Expenses
AB Foundation	2/5/2015	$200,245.29	Overhead and Staff Expenses
AB Foundation	2/5/2015	$20,249.84	Overhead and Staff Expenses
AB Foundation	2/25/2015	$192,000.00	Overhead and Staff Expenses
AB Foundation	3/20/2015	$33,685.32	Overhead and Staff Expenses
AB Foundation	3/20/2015	$18,635.06	Overhead and Staff Expenses
AB Foundation	4/2/2015	$250,481.89	Overhead and Staff Expenses
AB Foundation	6/30/2015	$30.00	Overhead and Staff Expenses
AB Foundation	6/30/2015	$351,225.45	Overhead and Staff Expenses

Contributor	Date	Amount	Purpose
AB Foundation	6/30/2015	$190,000.00	Overhead and Staff Expenses
AB Foundation	9/10/2015	$225,000.00	Overhead and Staff Expenses
AB Foundation	9/28/2015	$49,000.00	Overhead and Staff Expenses
AB Foundation	9/30/2018	$20,000.00	Overhead and Staff Expenses
AB Foundation	10/1/2015	$20,000.00	Overhead and Staff Expenses
AB Foundation	10/15/2015	$3,000.00	Overhead and Staff Expenses
AB Foundation	10/15/2015	$110,000.00	Overhead and Staff Expenses
AB Foundation	10/19/2015	$50,000.00	Overhead and Staff Expenses
AB Foundation	10/28/2015	$170,000.00	Overhead and Staff Expenses
AB Foundation	11/9/2015	$25,000.00	Overhead and Staff Expenses
AB Foundation	11/25/2015	$100,000.00	Overhead and Staff Expenses
AB Foundation	11/25/2015	$50,000.00	Overhead and Staff Expenses
AB Foundation	12/2/2015	$100,000.00	Overhead and Staff Expenses
AB Foundation	12/10/2015	$315,000.00	Overhead and Staff Expenses
AB Foundation	12/31/2015	$412,500.00	Overhead and Staff Expenses

It seems extremely unlikely the exact amount of employee hours worked would come out to such a round number as the $50,000 payment on April 4, 2014, the $100,000 payment on April 11, 2014, or the $50,000 payment on May 19, 2014. Maybe a typo, or sloppy accounting? Everything gets back to normal after that, for a little while. Payments from May through September look a lot more specific, and a lot more proper. Then it really cranks up again, with a $400,000 payment in October, and several round payments over the next few months in the hundreds of thousands of dollars.

Then, at some point in 2015, payments stop being specific altogether. Every payment from June 30 through the end of the year has a round, general appearance. Remember, these payments are supposed to be specific reimbursements for specific expenses incurred—in this case, shared employees between the two organizations. The round payments look a lot more like donations than expense reimbursements. Indeed, Kerr demonstrates many of these payments exactly match donations made to the Foundation.[21] Remember, the super PAC must disclose the identities of its donors, but the Foundation can withhold the identities of its donors. If Brock has created a scheme to shield the identity of donors to the super PAC by transferring the donations directly from the Foundation, it would constitute an FEC violation by the Foundation. It would also potentially jeopardize the tax-exempt statuses of both organizations with the IRS.

Of course, AB Foundation stated in their application for tax-exempt status to the IRS they kept meticulous records of employee hours via time sheets. So they should have no problem proving these payments relate solely to expense reimbursements, and do not constitute donations. Right?

That's just the first layer of the complaint. "The second layer was looking at the rental agreements with Media Matters for America and all the other organizations," says Kerr. "Media Matters owns the office space at 455 Massachusetts Ave. They own the entire sixth floor. All these other organizations that share office space with them have rental agreements with Media Matters. The Franklin Forum, American Bridge, Correct the Record hybrid super PAC, they're all paying Media Matters rent because they're sharing office space."

However, Kerr notes a big discrepancy here. "Media Matters is not reporting that income to the IRS," he says. "Those dollars need to be reported. Every single year Media Matters reports zero dollars. They've hidden millions of dollars from the IRS. They've received money in sublet rental income and they're not reporting it."

Kerr says American Bridge also has problems reporting their income and expenses at the state level, in the states that require them to report such detail. "On American Bridge Foundation's audited financial statements," says Kerr, "I was only able to locate two years. The July 2013 through June 2014 tax year, and their short tax year, July 2014 through December 2014. Those are the only two audited financial statements I was able to find. They haven't reported any of the other ones to the states where they're required to report. In those documents they're reporting sublet payments to Media Matters. However, Media Matters doesn't report that income as received. Both Correct the Record super PAC and American Bridge 21st Century super PAC are sending hundreds of thousands of dollars to Media Matters per month in rent. You can look it up on the FEC website."

The third layer of the complaint, and what makes Media Matters look so brazen in their disregard for reporting requirements and coordination of efforts among their different related entities, concerns The Blueprint. The Plan to Kick Donald Trump's Ass, detailed in the previous chapter, caused deep concerns for Kerr. "It's very hard to get somebody to care about why it matters that Media Matters isn't reporting income," he says. "It's a challenge to connect the two, because they don't understand what Media Matters does and the impact they have on our public discourse. I don't want to come out and say that political nonprofits or nonprofits that have a partisan leaning shouldn't be able to interact with journalists. My concern with Media Matters is their strategy for confronting ideas they don't agree with is to silence those ideas—not to actively engage with them."

Kerr expressed particular concern at the revelation in The Blueprint that Media Matters was working directly with social media companies and gaining access to their raw user data. "When I saw that they were working directly with Facebook and gaining raw access to people's information, it's one thing to be going after public figures. They understand, 'Hey, I'm entering politics,' or 'I'm a journalist, I'm entering the public sphere. I'm open to receiving criticism.'" Kerr thinks private citizens should be subject to a different standard. He says, "Just a run-of-the-mill citizen engaging in arguments on social media is not agreeing to that social contract. So to have a behemoth like Media Matters come in and strong-arm them and try to get them removed just for expressing an opinion, that's kind of the culture that organizations like Media Matters have helped cultivate, and I think that's bad for public discourse. If it turns out that these organizations appear to be breaking disclosure laws to the IRS and the FEC, they should be held accountable for that."

Luckily, Kerr had some flexibility in his schedule. He says, over a period of about three weeks, he put in sixteen-hour days just poring over the Form 990s, audited financial reports to secretaries of states, and other financial documents for all of the Brock entities.

Then he had to find a lawyer who would take the case, take the time understand the nature of the problem, and help him organize his thoughts into an FEC complaint that actually made sense. "The supporting documentation for all this was two binders full of paperwork, double-sided printing," Kerr says. "I printed it all out because it's much more easy to explain this. You have all these documents that are talking to one another, these forty-page documents, and it's one line in a document that talks to another line on another forty-page document. When you link those two together, and you have to link a couple other pieces together, that's how you piece the story together." That complexity caused Kerr to have to make some decisions. He says, "It does take a while to properly explain it because there are so many factors. There is a number of things that I covered with my lawyers that didn't make it into the complaint."

With this level of meticulous detail, the meeting with the lawyers took a while. "We had a seven-hour meeting going back and forth," says Kerr. "We had a lot of healthy debate with determining what should be in this thing and what shouldn't." Kerr laughs at how much time he took with the lawyers, saying, "They made the mistake of giving me a flat rate. I don't think they understood how complicated this was."

What resulted from the meeting and subsequent consultations is a damning complaint. It includes five separate charges (taken directly from the complaint itself):[22]

1. During 2013–2017, and perhaps beginning earlier, AB Foundation and AB Super PAC implemented procedures which appear to have resulted in the evasion of the requirements of federal law requiring the disclosure of contributors to AB Super PAC by establishing a system whereby contributions earmarked for or intended for AB Super PAC would be made in the first instance to AB Foundation and then transferred by AB Foundation to AB Super PAC as purported operating expenses (such as "Overhead & Staff Expenses") pursuant to a "common paymaster" arrangement.

2. Respondent AB Foundation...appears to have made payments to respondent AB Super PAC that were not payments for "Overhead & Staff Expenses," but were in fact contributions used to fund political activities. If so, respondent AB Foundation acted—in its own stead or as a co-venturer with AB Super PAC—as a political committee, and was required to register and report its activities as such. For example, funding the preparation of the Trump Accountability Project reports, described *supra*, was for the purpose of funding political activities. A political committee's failure to register and report as a political committee violates FECA and FEC regulations.

3. Improper utilization of the common paymaster arrangement described above in paragraphs 5–9 would result in incorrect reporting of contributions from AB Foundation to AB Super PAC as "Overhead & Staff Expenses." Failure to correctly report contributions received appears to violate 52 U.S.C. § 30104(b) and 11 C.F.R. § 102.9, 104.7, 104.8. *See, e.g.*, Exhibit F hereto (AB Super PAC's 2015 January 31 Year-End Form 3X (7/1/15 through 12/31/15), as amended on August 31, 2016, pp. 1–5). This failure also would have resulted in any number of reporting violations by AB Super PAC, some of which are indicated above, and others of which may become manifest from the FEC's investigation. Employees of both AB Foundation and AB Super PAC should have been required to maintain detailed employee time records, and procedures should have been put in place for the appropriate allocation of expenses by shared employees of both organizations.

4. In its January 31 Year-End FEC Form 3X (7/1/15 through 12/31/15), as amended on August 31, 2016, AB Super PAC reported that it had no indebtedness to AB Foundation, while AB Foundation's 2015 Form 990 reported that AB Super PAC was indebted to AB Foundation in the amount of $610,800.

5. CR Hybrid PAC failed to report the receipt of a valuable email list received in late 2015. It appears that CR Hybrid PAC received use of the email list owned

by Ready PAC, formerly known as "Ready for Hillary PAC," in late 2015. *See* attachment (titled "CTR Update. docx") to email of M. Bonner, dated December 1, 2015, https://wikileaks.org/podesta-emails/emailid/5636. This attachment—a memorandum which, *inter alia*, recounted recent political efforts of CR Hybrid PAC— detailed the fact that CR Hybrid PAC had widely used the Ready PAC (formerly "Ready for Hillary PAC") email list in late 2015:

6. SPREADING THE MESSAGE: Over 15,000 individuals receive Correctors emails, urging them to engage on social media to amplify Correct The Record's message in real time as an online rapid-response team. Correct The Record has also sent emails to the larger Ready for Hillary list, which have been consumed more than 400,000 times.

The complaint is summarized at the end: "The Complainant, having searched the FEC reports filed by CR Hybrid PAC, has been unable to discover any FEC report filed by CR Hybrid PAC reporting receipt or use of the value of the email list or otherwise recognizing use of the list in any way. Assuming CR Hybrid PAC received the email list, failure to report the value of such a valuable in-kind contribution would appear to be a clear violation of federal law."

A hybrid PAC, otherwise known as a Carey Committee, is a new creation based on a decision in the United States District Court for the District of Columbia, *Carey v. the Federal Election*

Commission. According to the FEC, "A political committee that maintains one bank account for making contributions in connection with federal elections and a separate 'non-contribution account' for making independent expenditures. The first account is subject to all of the limits and prohibitions of the Act, but the non-contribution account may accept unlimited contributions from individuals, corporations, labor organizations and other political committees. The committee must register with the FEC and report all receipts and disbursements for both accounts."[23] This last bit is where Correct the Record appears to have tripped up, when they failed to report the receipt of the email list.

Back to number 4 for a moment: The fact AB Super PAC failed to report a debt of over $600,000 to AB Foundation cannot be explained away as a mere typo. That part of the complaint appears to be a slam dunk, and a significant violation which could cost the super PAC a large fine, or worse.

In fact, if Kerr succeeds on every point in this complaint—at the time of this writing, a significant What If—each organization could be subject to large fines, back tax bills, loss of tax-exempt status, perhaps even being forced to close up shop. Kerr even speculates, if these organizations were to lose their tax-exempt status, it could cause their donors to be liable for taxes on the donations which were improperly deducted in their personal tax filings. The complaint has yet to be investigated, so let's not put the cart before the horse just yet.

And yet, it becomes clear the more one digs into the dealings among all of Brock's organizations, an enormous artifice exists whose sole purpose is to obfuscate and shield donors, directors, employees, and the organizations themselves from public scrutiny.

Merriam-Webster defines laundering in reference to money: "to transfer (illegally obtained money or investments) through an outside party to conceal the true source."[24] Should Kerr's complaint succeed at the FEC, the transfers among all the Brock entities would perfectly fit the definition.

CHAPTER 3

GREENWASHING

The Extra-Legal Means
Used to Scrub Money and Influence
Environmental Policy

*"The liberties of a people never were, nor ever will
be, secure, when the transactions of their rulers may
be concealed from them."*

—PATRICK HENRY

The puppet masters of radical environmental campaigns conceal themselves by design, while granting the entire progressive movement the appearance of an organic, grass-roots uprising devoid of Wall Street and corporate interests. The romantic notion of a bottom-up, people-led, voice-of-the-little-guy movement in the nostalgic image of the protests of the 1960s is only so much veneer. They make false claims of the will of the people while hiding from the public their actions to influence policy. The progressive green movement more resembles The Great and Mighty Oz, controlled by the Man (or men) Behind the Curtain. The puppet masters consist of the very Wall Street interests the young idealists and rank and file Democrats claim to despise. They push their agenda by exploiting IRS codes surrounding nonprofit groups, creating PR campaigns to pressure corporations into acceding to their extreme demands, and exerting control over as many elected officials as they can. When none of that works, they engage in a sort of Kabuki Theater where they play a contrived David-versus-Goliath game, known as sue and settle, except they've already rigged the system. Their web of nonprofit organizations claims to be David but really is the Goliath—and they propel the movement with vast sums of money earned in ways progressive anti-capitalists despise. It doesn't take much to portray the big bad US government as the bad guy, but when one looks closely, it becomes obvious when they sue, they've already gamed the system by planting their friends in the very agencies they sue, making a settlement a foregone conclusion.

Of course, relative anonymity and the ability to shield the identities of donors to the cause confer a tremendous advantage to the puppet masters. We The People, too often, end up manipulated by the rich and powerful, if they pay any attention to us at all.

The number of ever-changing nonprofit front groups boggles the mind and defies an honest attempt to catalogue. The puppet masters deliberately exploit legal loopholes and deliberately conceal their true identities—and true motives. Picture an infinite shell game, or perhaps an infinity-card monte. While many people involved in the environmental movement firmly believe they are doing good for Mother Earth, many organizations they support skirt the law or violate it outright. Many cease to exist before regulators can investigate their activities. No method of subterfuge is off-limits: foreign contributions, influence peddling, money laundering, violations of IRS tax codes and campaign finance laws.

Even the legal and legitimate funding originates from many sources the Left professes to hate. A small sampling of the dark money behind funders on the radical Left includes predatory home lending (which led to the housing crash in 2008), hedge fund trading, investments in coal, Big Oil energy funds, Big Pharma and the opioid crisis, and many other industries believed by the Left to prey upon the poor and the disadvantaged, or otherwise participate in activities progressives claim to hate. Meanwhile, the corporations despised by the Left—and those who enrich themselves by trading their stocks—continue to gain ever more wealth off the backs of those true believers in the movement. Indeed, financial self-interest is often the biggest hidden influence buried at the bottom of these efforts.

As we've seen in other aspects of this web of influence, the movement relies on moving money around among groups, through layers of often anonymous grantmaking or soliciting fundraising. That's not to say these funds transfers amount to legally actionable money laundering, but if it walks like a duck, quacks like a duck, and swims on a pile of money like a duck, then it's certainly a member of the waterfowl family. In many cases, such as the Media Matters for America example cited in the previous chapter, significant enough questions exist to warrant further investigation. Further, naked attempts at directly buying influence project a brazenness and a complete disregard for the risks of being caught. This network of influence peddling and money laundering has already led to the downfall of one beloved progressive governor on the West Coast.

That governor, Democrat John Kitzhaber of Oregon, had an ambitious agenda. Along with creating a centerpiece of Obamacare's expansion of Medicaid, expanding cradle-to-college education, gun control, and repeal of the death penalty, Kitzhaber sought a legacy as a green governor. It was his girlfriend, however, who really pushed the green energy agenda. This agenda closely matched how the Obama White House wanted to transform the economy and energy utilization of the United States.

Remember when candidate Barack Obama said he would fundamentally transform America, and under his plan electricity costs would necessarily skyrocket? Turns out, these ideas weren't terribly popular with the American voting public. Obama didn't possess the superhuman force of will to get the American public on board with doubling or tripling their electricity and heating bills in the wake of the Great Recession—never mind convincing Congress. This forced Obama and his radical allies to explore alternatives. A network of nonprofits, resembling Organizing for America and MoveOn.org, pivoted to the state level. There, they found pockets of support

for their green energy scheme. Activists could more easily organize communities state by state, and could curry favor from the
Obama administration when they did.

So, advancing a green energy agenda for Oregon would
confer special favor on Kitzhaber and his crew. To advance his
green energy scheme, Governor Kitzhaber had an employee
placed in his office by an obscure environmental nonprofit
funded by billionaire hedge fund trader Tom Steyer.[1] Read
that again: *Kitzhaber employed a policy director who reported
directly to a third-party, out-of-state group intent on changing
state policy.* In addition, the twice-divorced Kitzhaber had a
live-in girlfriend, Cylvia Hayes, who ran an environmental consulting business out of the governor's mansion. Hayes received
fat payoffs in the form of consulting fees for her influence over
public policy by a similar environmental nonprofit, also funded
by Steyer and other major players.[2]

Due to this influence-peddling scheme, Kitzhaber, under
intense political and public pressure, resigned in February 2015,
a few months after winning a record fourth election as governor
of Oregon.[3]

This was no oversight, no mere mistake. Radical environmentalists deliberately advanced this scheme to place
employees directly in governor's offices, with the express intent
of creating and pushing green energy policies. It didn't just
happen in Oregon. At last count, at least a dozen states employed
such a scheme to hire someone to act as a direct conduit back
to the environmental puppet masters. Oddly, only in deep-blue

Oregon has the governor faced political consequences for this scheme—so far, at least.

The inner mechanics of this web of influence came to light shortly after Kitzhaber's resignation, in a 2015 report by Energy & Environment Legal Institute (E&E Legal), a sort of watchdog group of attorneys who research and strategically litigate the misdeeds of the environmental movement in America.[4] They had already caught wind of the scheme prior to Kitzhaber's resignation and had made dozens of public record requests from several states to examine the email communications between these environmental groups and state governments. After all, the government belongs to the people, and the people should have the right to understand all the influences on policy and policy makers. The report, authored by senior legal fellow Chris Horner, revealed this network deliberately placed employees in the offices of friendly governors, in order to get states to sign on to unpopular and expensive green energy standards. The regulations, designed to implement severe restrictions on state-level carbon emissions, were written by the extreme leftist groups founded and funded by Tom Steyer, George Soros, and other shadowy donors, coordinated with the Obama White House, and pushed by their plants in the governors' offices.[5]

In the case of Oregon, an environmental activist named Dan Carol became the highest-paid employee in the governor's office. In fact, Governor Kitzhaber created a position just for him: Director of the Office of Multi-State Initiatives. This occurred as a result of Carol arranging the high-paying consulting gig for Kitzhaber's live-in girlfriend, the aforementioned

Cylvia Hayes. Of course, Carol pled otherwise in interviews with the media, saying he was hired for his environmental expertise.[6] His salary, which greatly exceeded that of any other governor's staffer—and was almost double that of the governor himself—signals otherwise.

That gig Carol arranged paid Hayes well in excess of $200,000 in consulting fees over a period of a couple of years. A DC-based nonprofit called the Clean Economy Development Center (CEDC), paid those fees to Hayes in exchange for her efforts in shaping state policy and communications regarding green energy.[7] The IRS dissolved the CEDC shortly after the scandal broke, for failure to file the required tax reporting forms for nonprofit organizations (IRS form 990) for three consecutive years of operation.[8] Three people ran CEDC while it operated—an activist from Portland named Jeffrey King, a former Oregon legislator named Jules Bailey, and Cylvia Hayes. Each carried the title of Senior Fellow at CEDC.[9]

Astute readers will note, at this point, that Cylvia Hayes served as Senior Fellow at CEDC at the same time she received consulting fees from CEDC, at the same time she sought to increase her influence as "informal advisor" to her governor boyfriend.

For her part, Hayes forgot to report this income, and her governor boyfriend forgot to disclose it on state ethics forms disclosing sources of household income.[10] This second bit prompted a formal investigation by the Oregon Attorney General as well as by the federal Department of Justice. While those investigations were closed without charges, the Oregon

Government Ethics Commission released a series of reports in late 2017 which concluded that a preponderance of evidence showed Hayes committed twenty-two violations of state ethics laws.[11] She now faces hundreds of thousands of dollars in fines. Kitzhaber attempted to settle, but the Ethics Commission rejected a settlement negotiation which would have required a fine of only $1,000 and no admission of guilt. Instead, the commission ruled Kitzhaber committed ten violations of state ethics laws. One commission member said: "I think what we have here is a blatant disregard for the ethics laws of this state. This is a case study in what you are not supposed to do as a public official."[12]

One would think Dan Carol, the guy for whom Kitzhaber created the highest-paying position in the governor's office, would also have to face the music. After all, he got all the credit for creating the consulting gig for Hayes while she occupied the governor's mansion, and he also created the main points of the green energy agenda for Hayes to push.

Of course, it doesn't really work like that. Carol has landed on his feet in a similar position in the office of California Governor Jerry Brown.[13] You see, this green energy scheme, coordinated with Organizing for America and the Obama White House, bankrolled by Steyer and Soros and the Rockefeller Brothers Fund and Michael Bloomberg and the Hewlett Foundation, created this position to be replicated in as many governor's offices as possible, across the nation. This affords the radical environmental movement direct influence over policy makers, in the form of an unelected, unaccountable bureaucrat, bypassing state lobbying rules and limitations on influence peddling. The emails obtained by Chris Horner for the E&E Legal report bear this out.[14]

Not satisfied with this level of influence by an unelected outside interest, this network of extreme environmental groups has upped the ante in Washington state. In January 2018, Horner and the *Wall Street Journal* revealed a radical environmental group actually contracted with Governor Jay Inslee to employ a policy expert in his office, with the express purpose of advancing a green agenda.[15] The World Resources Institute (WRI), a 501(c)(3) with offices in Washington, DC, Brazil, Indonesia, China, and other locations around the world, and income just a hair under $100 million on their latest Form 990, actually hired the State of Washington on contract.[16]

This scheme bears a striking resemblance to the Dan Carol arrangement which paid Cylvia Hayes for her influence over Governor Kitzhaber in Oregon, and eventually led to his resignation under the cloud of ethics violations. In fact, the emails uncovered by Chris Horner of E&E Legal reveal the Obama White House referred approvingly to "Dan's Plan" to employ a "grown-up" in as many governor's offices as possible to advance a radical green agenda.[17]

"So it's okay if the Koch Foundation pays the salary of the Wyoming energy advisor?" Horner applies this simple test to determine whether the public should scrutinize such arrangements. In an interview, he said: "They're not the state. Does it matter if they're for-profit or a non-governmental organization? Because what I'm seeing is that this is allowed to be done for some donors, and they will do whatever the governors ask, including, also, pay for outside consultants to the governors. Just a mess."

If progressives really want to start getting the influence of dark money out of politics and public policy making, they may wish to start with Governor Inslee's office. After all, an outside entity not headquartered in the state of Washington pays the state to a) employ an unelected bureaucrat accountable only to that organization and not to the state, and b) produce measurable differences in state policy which they approve, bypassing the voters entirely. This arrangement actually takes the Kitzhaber affair, which cost him the governor's mansion and a likely sizeable fine, along with the loss of his reputation, and, as Nigel Tufnel of Spinal Tap would say, cranks it up to eleven.

So, what does the World Resources Institute do, and who funds them? Founded in 1982, WRI operates in over fifty nations and has a staff of over 450 that works with local leaders on natural resource issues.[18] With their enormous budget, they can afford to deploy policy experts in many layers of the public sphere. As a 501(c)(3), they regularly receive grants from other foundations, as well as government grants. According to their financial audit reports for 2015 and 2016, well over 50 percent of their budget consists of grants from foreign nations. The audit report gives the following breakdown of their grants from foreign governments on page 17:[19]

Grants, pledges and contracts receivable are recorded at their net realizable values. The mix of receivables as of September 30 was as follows:

	2016	2015
U.S. government	3%	4%
Foundations	6%	18%
Foreign governments	**56%**	**67%**
International organizations	20%	2%
Corporations, individuals, and others	15%	9%
	100%	100%

Now, most progressives at this point would chime in and say something along the lines of, "Hey, the environment is a global problem, it requires everyone on Earth to pitch in and make a difference." Nevertheless, the number of Washington voters cannot be very substantial who realize a bureaucrat in Governor Inslee's office has a heavy hand in creating state policy while the position gets at least some of its funding from grants from foreign governments.

Inslee has also taken aggressive steps to lead on climate on a national level, calling into further question whether he serves two masters—the voters of Washington and radical environmentalists. In response to President Trump's decision to leave the Paris Agreement on climate change, Governor Inslee partnered with Governor Jerry Brown of California and Governor Andrew Cuomo of New York to found and lead the US Climate Action Alliance. Currently, fourteen states and the territory of Puerto Rico have signed on as members.[20] Incidentally, Oregon also signed on, but current Governor Kate Brown—who, by all accounts, tilts further to the left than the deposed Kitzhaber—keeps a lower profile in the wake of the previous scandal.

The mission statement on the Climate Action Alliance website states:[21]

> "In response to the U.S. federal government's decision to withdraw the United States from the Paris Agreement, Governors Andrew Cuomo, Jay Inslee, and Jerry Brown launched the United States Climate Alliance—a bipartisan coalition of governors committed to reducing greenhouse gas emissions consistent with the goals of the Paris Agreement. Smart, coordinated state action can ensure that the United States continues to contribute to the global effort to address climate change."

The billionaires and their web of nonprofits didn't stop there, though. Indeed, the state-level manipulations are just small potatoes. The manipulations at the federal level dwarf the local attempts to hijack our republic. The model remains similar, though—place people into bureaucratic positions in governmental agencies who sympathize with the radical environmental movement, conduct large scale campaigns which target specific policies, and have this governmental official do everything they can to grease the skids to make that new policy a reality. All while avoiding any legislative oversight or accountability to the voters.

It really is hard to know where to start when describing this phenomenon as it exists at the federal level. The abuse is so widespread and so common, it defies an honest attempt to document it all. The Environmental Protection Agency provides three pernicious examples which point to systemic issues across the federal leviathan. At the end of the chapter, a bonus fourth example will be provided.

Example 1: The Billionaire's Club

The first example provided the impetus for a congressional investigation. A 2014 Minority Staff Report from the Senate Committee on Environment and Public Works went into great detail in describing the network of influencers at the Environmental Protection Agency (EPA).[22] In that report, they state bluntly, *"an elite group of left wing millionaires and billionaires, which this report refers to as the 'Billionaire's Club,' who directs and controls the far-left environmental movement, which in turn controls major policy decisions and lobbies on behalf of the U.S. Environmental Protection Agency (EPA). Even more unsettling, a dominant organization in this movement is Sea Change Foundation, a private California foundation, which relies on funding from a foreign company with undisclosed donors. In turn, Sea Change funnels tens of millions of dollars to other large but discreet foundations and prominent environmental activists who strive to control both policy and politics."[23] (emphasis added)*

This mirrors their state level attempts to control environmental and energy policies with radical agenda shifts to the far left.

The report lays out the network of influence, and how deep it goes. It further goes on to state, "The failure to openly acknowledge this force and the silence of the media with whom they coordinate further emphasize the fact that until today, the

Billionaire's Club operated in relative obscurity hidden under the guise of 'philanthropy.' The scheme to keep their efforts hidden and far removed from the political stage is deliberate, meticulous, and intended to mislead the public. While it is uncertain why they operate in the shadows and what they are hiding, what is clear is that these individuals and foundations go to tremendous lengths to avoid public association with the far-left environmental movement they so generously fund. The report attempts to decipher the patterns of 'charitable giving. Often the wealthiest foundations donate large sums to intermediaries—sometimes a pass through and sometimes a fiscal sponsor. The intermediary then funnels the money to other 501(c)(3) and 501(c)(4) organizations that the original foundation might also directly support. The report offers theories that could explain this bizarre behavior, but at its core, the Billionaire's Club is not, and seemingly does not, want to be transparent about the groups they fund and how much they are supporting them. In advancing their cause, these wealthy liberals fully exploit the benefits of a generous tax code meant to promote genuine philanthropy and charitable acts, amazingly with little apparent Internal Revenue Service scrutiny. Instead of furthering a noble purpose, their tax deductible contributions secretly flow to a select group of left wing activists who are complicit and eager to participate in the fee-for-service arrangement to promote shared political goals. Moreover, the financial arrangement provides significant insulation to these wealthy elite from the incidental damage they do to the U.S. economy and average Americans."[24]

Sounds familiar, no? As detailed in a previous chapter, David Brock and his various foundations—Media Matters for America, American Bridge 21st Century PAC, Franklin Forum, etc.—follow this exact model of a financial shell game and have had multiple complaints filed against them. The media have, so far, failed to notice.

The report refers to the "Billionaire's Club" and how its elite members "direct the far-left environmental movement." These wealthy individuals "funnel their fortunes through private foundations to execute their personal political agenda, which is centered around restricting the use of fossil fuels in the United States."[25] Herein lies the crux of the issue. A bottom-up movement simply would not exist without it being driven by the personal agendas and the phony reporting on the effects of their efforts. As the picture becomes clearer, it becomes evident the Billionaire's Club has gamed the entire system. The myriad foundations direct the activities of the "charities" to which they donate. The Club also funds scientific-sounding foundations to provide academic cover, and nonprofit journalistic watchdogs to ensure the media tells the story they want told. They don't simply donate to a nonprofit that does what they consider good work. It's all directed by a small group of wealthy elites.

Of course, as the Senate report notes, "Members of the Billionaire's Club also donate directly to 501(c)(3) public charities. Generally, the public charity is considered the preferred status under the tax code, based on the greater tax benefits and protections on donor disclosures."[26] Transparency and public accountability represent direct threats to their efforts.

The 2014 Senate report notes another aspect of the Club's attempt to control how their donations are used, saying, "Public charities attempt to provide the maximum amount of control to their donors through fiscal sponsorships, which are a legally suspect innovation unique to the left, whereby the charity actually sells its nonprofit status to a group for a fee."[27] A sponsorship allows an organization to "borrow" the nonprofit status of an affiliated group to gather tax-deductible donations under the rules governing 501(c)(3)s. Sponsorships are intended to be temporary and must benefit an organization with operations substantially similar to those of the sponsoring foundation.

One example the report cites, Bill McKibben's 350.org, held a sponsorship from the Sustainable Markets Foundation (SMF) for several years. How radical are Bill McKibben and 350.org? Read the statement from their website:

> "350 uses online campaigns, grassroots organizing, and mass public actions to oppose new coal, oil and gas projects, take money out of the companies that are heating up the planet, and build 100% clean energy solutions that work for all. 350's network extends to 188 countries."[28]

It is no exaggeration to say 350.org and the Keep It In The Ground movement advocate for nothing less than the complete abandonment of carbon-based fuel sources.

SMF sponsors many more equally radical environmental organizations, allowing them to avoid all that burdensome reporting paperwork with the FEC and the IRS. The reason to suspect these sponsorship arrangements, according to the report, is they were built on a very obscure precedent from half a century ago. They note the IRS originally wrote the rule for temporary projects, saying, "it should be in the context of 'specific short term project[s]—such as providing assistance following a local disaster, or construction of a new playground or dog park.'" They continue, saying, "However, in the realm of the far-left environmental movement, fiscal sponsorship arrangements are far from temporary and usually around for several years or more. One fiscal sponsorship arrangement has existed for over 23 years, and the sponsored entity has indicated no plans to properly establish its own nonprofit status."[29]

Among the far-left activist environmental set, the number of fiscal sponsorships has expanded significantly in the past decade and a half. The Senate report notes nonprofits on the Right rarely emulate this practice.[30]

The Billionaire's Club report also takes a deep dive into the phenomenon of prescriptive grantmaking. No longer do the largest foundations in the radical environmental movement accept unsolicited grant requests. "Don't call us, we'll call you," they say right on their websites. For instance, the Environmental Grantmakers Association website states in its FAQ section: "Q: I need a grant. Can you help me? A: Unfortunately, EGA does not have the capacity to help grantseekers at this time. We suggest you visit these helpful links."[31] The Rockefeller Brothers Fund website puts it more directly: "While the Fund remains open to unsolicited requests, applicants should be aware that the likelihood of an unsolicited request becoming a grant is low."[32]

Why would these massive foundations, with virtually limitless resources they could dedicate to changing the world, reject unsolicited grant requests? Quite simply, so they can control what the money does once it's granted. As the Billionaire's Club report says: "Public charity activist groups propagate the false notion that they are independent, citizen-funded groups working altruistically. In reality, they work in tandem with wealthy donors to maximize the value of the donors' tax-deductible donations and leverage their combined resources to influence elections and policy outcomes, with a focus on the U.S. Environmental Protection Agency (EPA)."[33] This means the Club pours its money into a large network of nonprofits which engage in all sorts of tactics—lobbying, lawsuits, and grassroots organizing to create public pressure on bureaucrats. In turn for this financial largesse, this network of groups does the bidding of the Club.

This bidding includes a custom-built echo chamber. In a sort of perpetual-motion machine of influence and money, favor gets transferred in a giant cycle. "Former far-left environmentalists working at EPA funnel government money through grants to their former employers and colleagues," according to the report, "often contributing to the bottom line of environmental activist groups."[34] The Senate report, authored while President Obama occupied the White House, takes special note of the incestuous relationships between activist groups, former activists now in bureaucratic roles, and the special favors shared back and forth. "Under President Obama, EPA has given more than $27 million in taxpayer-funded grants to major environmental groups. Notably, the Natural Resources Defense

Council and Environmental Defense Fund—two key activists groups with significant ties to senior EPA officials—have collected more than $1 million in funding each."[35]

The Billionaire's Club also funds the support apparatus to get the public to buy in, or at least to ignore these incestuous relationships, with full-fledged propaganda operations pushing out questionable science commissioned by the Club to come up with a desired result. A particularly devastating passage in the report demonstrates the Club pays for foundations to provide this kind of support: "Some of the most valued services activists provide the Billionaire's Club includes promulgation of propaganda, which creates an artificial echo chamber; appearance of a faux grassroots movement; access to nimble and transient groups under fiscal sponsorship arrangements; distance/anonymity between donations made by well-known donors and activities of risky activist groups; and above all—the ability to leverage tens of millions of dollars in questionable foreign funding."[36]

We'll address the foreign funding in a later chapter. Meanwhile, what propaganda does this apparatus advance? In many cases, they push phony science and misleading stats taken out of context to create the impression of an imminent climate crisis. "Foundations finance research to justify desired predetermined policy outcome," they report. "The research is then reported on by a news outlet, oftentimes one that is also supported by the same foundation, in an effort to increase visibility. In one example, a story reporting on a Park Foundation-supported anti-fracking study was reproduced by a Park-funded news organization through a Park-funded media collaboration where it was then further disseminated on Twitter by the maker of Park-backed anti-fracking movies."[37]

One could be excused for thinking this no longer goes on in the Trump administration. Unfortunately, the Deep State continues to operate unabated, and the junk science and propaganda continue to get pumped out. Many of the Obama-era bureaucrats continue to hold their positions in the EPA. President Trump has his work cut out for him to drain the EPA swamp—especially in the wake of the resignation by his original pick to head the agency, Scott Pruitt.

Before his resignation, Pruitt made good progress. He ruled the agency would no longer use unverified science which can't be reproduced in rulemaking (more on that later in this chapter). Pruitt had a combative history of suing the EPA as Oklahoma's Attorney General prior to taking over. In that role, he sued the EPA over the Clean Power Plan advocated by the Obama administration, along with suing over methane emission restrictions. His replacement, Andrew Wheeler, has quite a way to go, however, in rooting out the holdovers who still surreptitiously work with the Billionaire's Club. Indeed, Pruitt's forced resignation was designed to slow down the process.

Example 2: John Beale, and the Particulate Pollutants Rule

The second EPA example involves a little-known bureaucrat, a gigantic whopper of a series of lies, faked science hidden from public scrutiny, and one of the most devastating regulations ever put in place by the agency. What flowed from this regulation shaped two decades of how rules were made at EPA, cost the United States economy untold billions in lost productivity, and caused one of the most embarrassing scandals in the history of the agency—and yet another Senate committee investigation and report.

John Beale was, by all accounts, a nobody. Though he had multiple advanced degrees, as an adult he drifted between jobs. According to the United States Senate Committee on Environment and Public Works Minority Staff Report of March 2014, Beale had "no clear career trajectory" after working in a small-town law firm, on various political campaigns, as a physical therapist, and even for a time on an apple farm.[38] Considering his best friend, Robert Brenner, hired him at an "abnormally high" starting salary to join him at EPA, you'd think he possessed some sort of scientific skill set or relevant policy experience. You would, of course, be wrong. Beale had very little relevant expertise. That didn't stop college chum Brenner from hiring him in 1989. Over the years, career bureaucrat Brenner had ascended through the ranks at EPA to the position of director of the Office of Policy, Analysis, and Review (OPAR) within the Office of Air and Radiation (OAR). For the first ten years of Beale's employment at EPA, he reported directly to his best friend Brenner. Brenner hired Beale as an entry-level policy analyst at a salary reserved for employees with twenty years of relevant experience.

In this director position, Brenner and his sidekick, Beale, expanded the duties and responsibilities of OPAR to the point that staff routinely referred to it as their fiefdom within EPA.[39] In the mid-1990s, they used this office to run point on the EPA's effort to set National Ambient Air Quality Standards (NAAQS). As the Senate report describes it, "The duo set in motion 'EPA's Playbook,' a strategy to game the system by compressing the Office of Information and Regulatory Affairs (OIRA) review via a friendly sue-and-settle arrangement, relying on secret science, and inflating benefits while underestimating costs."[40] It goes on to say, "With these standards, EPA sought to regulate fine particulates ($PM_{2.5}$) in addition to larger particles (PM_{10}) for the first time under the NAAQS, despite a distinct lack of scientific understanding of the integrity of the underlying data." Fine particulates are tiny particles in the air, not visible to the naked eye, which supposedly affect air quality. The 2.5 refers to their size, 2.5 microns or smaller—hence $PM_{2.5}$. PM_{10} refers to particulates of a larger size, 10 microns or smaller. These new rules would be the first time the federal government had ever regulated particulate matter in the atmosphere.

The Senate report outlines the problems with the processes used by EPA to come to their conclusion. It describes the process as Machiavellian, lining up just enough information to come to a predetermined conclusion:

"These circumstances were compounded by EPA's 'policy call' to regulate $PM_{2.5}$ for the first time in 1997. $PM_{2.5}$ are ubiquitous tiny particles, the reduction of which EPA used to support both the PM and Ozone NAAQS. In doing so, the Playbook also addressed Beale's approach to EPA's economic analysis: overstate the benefits and underrepresent the costs of federal regulations. This technique has been applied over the years and burdens the American people today, *as up to 80 percent of the benefits associated with all federal regulations are attributed to supposed PM2.5 reductions.*

"EPA has also manipulated the use of $PM_{2.5}$ through the NAAQS process as the proffered health effects attributable to $PM_{2.5}$ have never been independently verified. In the 1997 PM NAAQS, EPA justified the critical standards on only two data sets...[a]t the time, the underlying data for the studies were over a decade old and were vulnerable to even the most basic scrutiny. Yet the use of such weak studies reveals another lesson from EPA's Playbook: shield the underlying data from scrutiny."[41] (emphasis added)

Long story short, the EPA delayed and denied access to the underlying data for so long, it could not be recreated with sufficient fidelity to reproduce the results of the studies. A fundamental precept of the scientific method every first-year college student in the sciences learns is that an experiment must be able to be reproduced for its results to be considered valid. When that becomes impossible, the conclusions drawn from the experiment must be thrown out. Not so at the EPA, however, as those NAAQS from the 1990s continue today as the law of the land. Many other layers of regulations have had their basis in the regulation of particulate matter, and many other regulations have used this exact model to find acceptance in the EPA.

Around this time, Beale also began telling an absolute whopper of a lie, revealing himself as a compulsive liar. This guy actually began telling people he led a double life and also worked undercover for the CIA. His compulsive lying led to a preferred parking spot after a phony story about contracting malaria in Vietnam, years upon years of failing to report to work and using the excuse he "had to go to Langley (CIA headquarters)," and finally, to his getting busted for taking a retention bonus of 25 percent of his salary for a dozen years, a bonus normally reserved for indispensable staff with unique skills, and only allowed in any case for a maximum of three years. It is difficult to see how that last bit could have happened without the complicity of his boss and best friend, Robert Brenner, according to the Senate report. Beale ended up convicted of defrauding the federal government out of almost $1 million in overpaid salary, although some estimate the total fraud to have been far higher. He served thirty-two months in federal prison. Though he retired in disgrace, Beale's legacy actually lives on in the form of what the Senate report calls the EPA Playbook.

Example 3: Sue and Settle

The third example revolving around the EPA revealed coordination between nonprofit foundations and their donors, friendly bureaucrats at the federal level, and lawyers who seek out sympathetic judges in federal courts—affectionately nicknamed "judge-shopping." Sue and Settle has become standard practice for the progressive foundations and radical environmental activists, and it had its ignominious start in the EPA Playbook devised by Beale and Brenner.

In 1997, as they wrangled to create the particulate matter regulations, Beale and Brenner faced significant pushback on the rulemaking for NAAQS. The simultaneous attempt to create regulations on both $PM_{2.5}$ and $PM_{10,}$ along with ozone, put significant pressure on OPAR. This pressure was compounded by a court-ordered timeframe that was much shorter than in a typical EPA rulemaking processes. The American Lung Association (ALA) had sued EPA to force them to implement the rules. This appears to be the first instance of Sue and Settle, which has sadly become commonplace among radical foundations on the progressive left. The Senate report describes the process in which friendly plaintiffs sue the agency and agree to settle on mutually agreeable terms. These terms are negotiated behind closed doors, away from the scrutiny of voters or their representatives. Not exactly the adversarial relationship envisioned in a plaintiff-versus-defendant judicial system. The negotiated settlement, according to the Senate report, resulted in a shoddy process which failed to rely on good science:

"In the case of the 1997 NAAQS, the ALA lawsuit resulted in a consent decree ordering EPA to propose standards for PM by November 29, 1996, and to issue final standards by July 19, 1997. The consent decree was silent on the deadline for Ozone NAAQS. When EPA sent the proposed standards to the Office of Management and Budget (OMB) for review on November 4,

1996, the proposal included not just standards for PM, but ozone as well. EPA was not required to reconsider the ozone standard until 1998, since the Agency had just completed a review of ozone in 1993. However, it appears Beale and Brenner made a 'policy call' and determined the Agency should propose standards for ozone in conjunction with the PM standards, which were subject to the court-imposed deadline. In proposing the Ozone and PM NAAQS in tandem, many scientific and analytical uncertainties were overlooked or deliberately ignored to comply with the compressed timeline."[42]

This pattern has repeated itself countless times in the two decades since. This remains the EPA Playbook to this day, and it all goes back to a college buddy hiring a compulsive-liar friend to help him run an unaccountable governmental agency with less and less oversight as the years went by.

BONUS Example #4: The Consumer Financial Protection Bureau

This example doesn't involve the EPA, but it deserves mention in a chapter dedicated to unaccountable bureaucrats funneling enormous sums of money to leftist causes out of a slush fund.

The Consumer Financial Protection Bureau (CFPB) was the brainchild of Elizabeth Warren when she was a professor at Harvard, prior to her election to the US Senate. She and her Democratic brethren believed that financial services industries in America were too under-regulated, and in the Great Recession, they got their chance to prove their point. It became law in the Dodd-Frank Wall Street Reform and Consumer Protection Act of 2010.[43] The Democratic majority in Congress granted the CFPB sweeping powers to regulate financial entities with almost no congressional oversight.[44] The CFPB has grown since its inception to involve itself in regulating auto loans, credit reporting agencies, credit and collections law, student loans, credit unions, and even school accreditation. This is on top of its original intent to regulate banks, lenders, credit card companies and other such financial institutions in the wake of the financial meltdown of 2008.[45]

The result? According to a report in the *New York Post* in December 2017, the resulting explosion of regulations and enforcement led to thousands of small lenders being forced out of business, and a giant new revenue stream in the form of fines levied on businesses that got crosswise with CFPB.[46] The *Post* report lists the greatest abuses committed by the CFPB during the Obama administration:

- Bounced business owners and industry reps from secret meetings it's held with Democrat operatives, radical civil rights activists, trial lawyers and other "community advisers," according to a report by the House Financial Services Committee.

- Retained GMMB, the liberal advocacy group that created ads for the Obama and Hillary Clinton presidential campaigns, for more than $40 million, making the Democrat shop the sole recipient of CFPB's advertising expenditure, Rubin says.

- Met behind closed doors to craft financial regulatory policy with notorious bank shakedown groups who have taken hundreds of thousands of dollars in federal grant money to gin up housing and lending discrimination complaints, which in turn are fed back to CFPB, according to Investor's Business Daily and Judicial Watch.

- Funneled a large portion of the more than $5 billion in penalties collected from defendants to community organizers aligned with Democrats—"a slush fund by another name," said a consultant who worked with CFPB on its Civil Penalty Fund and requested anonymity.[47]

That five billion-dollar slush fund comes with very few strings, and a strongly partisan bias. CFPB collects civil penalties and deposits them into the Civil Penalty Fund. This fund is then used for one of two purposes: reimbursing victims, or if victims cannot be reasonably compensated, consumer education. The consumer education portion has almost no oversight or guidance as to how it gets spent. The Competitive Enterprise Institute put it plainly in a 2016 report about CFPB, saying, "Yet in another example of how the Bureau's unconstitutional structure and lack of oversight corrupts its mission, it appears the CFPB has abused its power to penalize lawbreakers to establish a fund it has used for political purposes."[48]

In all these examples, we see clear efforts by unelected bureaucrats to create structures within governmental agencies.

They use these structures to shield their activities from public scrutiny. They then feel free to transfer money, exert influence, and change public policy ever leftward—all without the voters knowing or approving of the inexorable growth of the regulatory state.

CHAPTER 4

BEHIND THE CURTAIN

Who Drives the Agenda?

"A hypocrite despises those whom he deceives, but has no respect for himself. He would make a dupe of himself too, if he could."

—WILLIAM HAZLITT

By all accounts, the Climate Alliance will continue to follow the model explained in the previous chapter, by which they place bureaucrats in governors' offices who help coordinate state-level activities to create policy, again without accountability to the voters of the various states in which they operate. This arrangement really only scratches the surface of the crooked dealings in the vast network of dirty money in progressive politics. While "Dan's Plan" gives us an illustrative example, it only constitutes one small corner of the jigsaw puzzle. For a more complete picture, we need to examine the really big players in the radical environmentalist movement.

Let's take a deep dive into some of the most prolific donors, where their money goes, and their agenda for fundamentally changing America.

The radical Left has an agenda, make no mistake. It is formulated, propagated, and implemented by a series of ultra-wealthy individuals and foundations. They deliberately make it difficult to connect the dots, understand who pulls what strings, and see the ultimate goal. The donors and foundations also have the advantage of using IRS codes governing nonprofits to direct significant resources to charities, educational foundations, and philanthropic organizations which then engage in political activity.

Of course, they present themselves as philanthropists, generous men and women who have dedicated their wealth to the arts, education, social programs, and other noble causes. This philanthropy acts as something of a smokescreen to allow donors a measure of public goodwill. It also acts as misdirection from their more controversial contributions in the political realm.

The hypocrisy doesn't end with the veneer of altruism. Often, the stated goal of their political involvement masks a less altruistic motivation, namely profit.

Here's a breakdown of some of the biggest progressive donors and foundations and how they conduct their nonprofit work.

That picture begins with billionaire hedge fund manager Tom Steyer and his wife, Kat Taylor, but it extends far beyond even their influence, into a network of their billionaire buddies who choose to keep a lower profile.

The Whales

TOM STEYER

Steyer burst onto the progressive donor scene in 2010 when he and Kat Taylor signed the Giving Pledge, the effort by Warren Buffet and Bill Gates to get wealthy individuals to commit to donating half their net worth to charity within their lifetimes.[1] Steyer has always been involved in Democratic politics, but he has really ramped it up over the past decade or so. TomKat, as he and his wife have come collectively to be known, are familiar to many political junkies who are concerned with money and influence in American politics, but few realize the extent to which their influence has spread.

Steyer became a partner with Democracy Alliance, the group of progressive donors which meets semiannually to plan its giving projects.[2] DA requires its partners to donate a minimum of $200,000 per year to approved groups on the Left.[3] George Soros co-founded the DA in 2005, and the group includes a large number of members from the San Francisco Bay Area.[4] Steyer also has his hand in David Brock's Democracy Matters, another network of progressive donors that funds radical organizations and campaigns on the Left.[5] In addition,

Steyer actively participates in the Environmental Grantmakers Association.[6] He founded NextGen Climate Action, with a super PAC arm and a 501(c)(4) arm.[7]

Steyer has routinely ranked among the biggest individual donors to political campaigns since his involvement began, along with pouring massive amounts into nonprofit organizations. According to OpenSecrets.org, Steyer made it to Number One on the charts in 2016, donating $91,069,795 to liberal causes and campaigns in 2016.[8] For the sake of comparison, Sheldon Adelson, the top conservative donor, ranked number two overall, with $82 million donated, while George Soros placed a distant twelfth, donating a mere $22 million.[9]

Steyer's influence extends in multiple layers of government and politics. His super PAC, NextGen Climate Solutions, produced an extensive environmental policy statement which, according to multiple reports, found its way into the party platform adopted at the Democratic National Convention in 2016.[10] This happened, of course, after NextGen contributed nearly a million dollars to the Democratic National Committee to help pay for the convention. He also gave generously to Barack Obama's reelection campaign in 2012, holding fundraisers in his home where Obama appeared as the guest of honor.

Personally, Steyer made his wealth as a hedge fund manager. He founded Farallon Capital Management after having learned at the knee of future Treasury Secretary Robert Rubin at Goldman Sachs.[11] Though Steyer left as senior managing partner of Farallon in 2012 and semi-retired, he still maintains a role at the firm he founded, described by the *New Yorker* as a "limited partner role."[12] This relationship caused some to question his dedication to the environment when Farallon's investment in Kinder Morgan came to light. Kinder Morgan is a pipeline company with a line that competed with the Keystone XL pipeline, a favorite target of Steyer's. Steyer subsequently directed Farallon to divest all of its holdings in what he termed, "dirty energy." Steyer's personal holdings, along with those of Farallon, have since gone more and more toward the green energy sector. Thus, it stands to reason he still has the potential for a significant financial windfall if his public policy work leads to regulations which more strongly favor the industries in which he chose to invest.

This wasn't the first time Steyer and Farallon faced accusations of taking profits derived from questionable sources. In a 2013 article, "A Green Billionaire's Dirty Money," the Washington Free Beacon detailed Farallon's extensive history of investing in projects in which Steyer also had a political stake.[13] This history includes Farallon's investment in a project in Russia that would have helped privatize up to two hundred thousand companies after the fall of the Soviet Union and the turn to a capitalist society. Several US officials were investigated over their use of insider knowledge to profit from the scheme, as was Farallon, which ended up paying a seven-figure fine.

KAT TAYLOR

The other half of TomKat, Steyer's wife has her own career in activism and making money in an industry which takes advantage of favorable governmental regulations. With her husband, Kat co-founded Beneficial State Bank, an institution that provides financial services in economically depressed neighborhoods. These community banks receive federal funding from the US Treasury, under the Community Development Financial Institution Fund.[14]

Beneficial State Bank states all its profits become donations to a nonprofit foundation that works in the local community.[15] Oddly, the OpenSecrets.org website shows Beneficial State Bank donated $369,890 to federal candidates in 2016, 100 percent to liberals.[16]

Together, Taylor and Steyer founded TomKat Charitable Trust, which by all appearances, exists solely to accept personal donations from the couple to be doled out as grants to other organizations.

GEORGE SOROS

George Soros has occupied the main radar screen of conservatives for a couple of decades, and for good reason. Since he first founded his Open Society Institute in 1979, the institute has spent around $14 billion, and Soros himself has donated upwards of $30 billion[17] The amount of money that flows from his Open Society Foundations to every radical cause imaginable boggles the mind and defies a succinct attempt to catalog.

Soros, like Steyer, made his money as a hedge fund manager. In fact, so successful was Soros that in 2008, the Hedge Fund Manager's Hall of Fame made him a member of their inaugural class.[18]

A founding member of the Democracy Alliance, Soros also spends a lot of time and money with David Brock as a funder for many of his efforts—including the donor gathering during Inauguration Weekend 2017 to discuss the Plan to Kick Trump's Ass.

Soros has found himself in hot water in his international meddlings. His Open Society Foundations network has faced accusations that their involvement in the Middle East has created, or at least contributed to the refugee crisis faced by European nations.[19] In addition, according to Judicial Watch, another Soros foundation has used American taxpayer dollars to influence elections and boost left-wing activities in at least one European country. Through a Freedom of Information Act request, Judicial Watch found that the US Agency for International Development under the Obama administration provided $9 million to fund the Justice for All campaign in Albania, administered by the Soros-funded East-West Management Institute.[20] Judicial Watch continues to investigate Soros's activities in Cuba, Macedonia, Romania, Columbia, and other countries.

More details about the philosophy and political involvement of OSF can be found in the Appendix.

MICHAEL BLOOMBERG

Bloomberg began his career as an equity trader for a Wall Street bank, before being laid off in 1981. He then created a company, Bloomberg LP, which provides sophisticated data to trading firms to guide their trading decisions. His net worth has grown to over $50 billion, and he's actively engaged in politics for almost two decades.[21] He served three terms as mayor of New York City, and has since attacked public health issues, most times by attempting to apply heavy-handed public policy solutions that involve some mix of onerous regulation and punishing taxes. He's famous for pushing soda taxes in states and municipalities all over the country, and pressing for oppressive gun restrictions. He founded the Bloomberg Family Foundation, which has annual income at or above $1 billion.[22] The Bloomberg Family Foundation, in turn, funds Everytown for Gun Safety, an anti-gun nonprofit with the goal of radically reducing gun rights in America.[23]

HERB SANDLER

Herb Sandler (and his wife, Marion, before she passed) doesn't make the news with anywhere near the frequency of Steyer, Soros, or Bloomberg. Nonetheless, they wield tremendous power in the progressive donor class. Sandler made his fortune by creating a bank, Golden West Financial Corporation. Their bank branches, numbering 285 throughout the Western United States at their peak, operated under the name World Savings Bank. They sold the organization to Wachovia Bank in 2006 and took home a cool $2.4 billion for their troubles.

Of course, the rosy depiction of an affable husband-and-wife team that built up a family business takes on a different hue when it becomes clear this acquisition doomed Wachovia to failure.[24] The acquisition happened right at the peak of the housing bubble, right before the burst caused the 2008 Great

Recession. Golden West had pioneered several alternative types of loans such as "Pick-a-pay" and other sub-prime lending practices.[25] The Sandlers have also faced criticism for loosening lending standards in the years leading up to their planned retirement, in order to inflate the value of the asset they sold to Wachovia. The failure of Wachovia, based in large part on the toxic loan portfolio they acquired from Golden West, was one of the main dominoes to fall that accelerated the recession. Wachovia was the fourth-largest bank in America at the time, and its failure signaled greater problems in the home lending industry.

Because of the outsized effect their portfolio had on the entire US banking industry after the acquisition, Golden West famously earned the nickname, "the Typhoid Mary of the housing crisis." Herb Sandler has faced personal criticism as well, earning the label of most evil billionaire in the world.[26, 27]

Herb and Marion Sandler took their ill-gotten wealth and poured it into a large network of progressive causes. Herb co-founded the Center for American Progress with John Podesta. He also founded ProPublica, a foundation which supports supposedly independent journalism but skews hard to the left in its coverage. Sandler's position of Founding Chair of ProPublica came after a series of initial donations in excess of $30 million.[28] Sandler has also lavishly supported Steyer's NextGen Climate Action Fund. Coincidentally, Steyer's wife, Kat Taylor, serves on the board of directors for ProPublica.

Even before they became billionaires, Herb and Marion Sandler had the wherewithal to support liberal political causes.

According to OpenSecrets.org, they were the number-one individual donors in America during the 2004 election cycle. That year, they gave $2.5 million to MoveOn.org and several million more to the liberal group Citizens for a Strong Senate. The non-profit they created, the Sandler Foundation, is another outfit which does not award unsolicited grants. Created in 1991, the Sandler Foundation saw a massive influx of cash fifteen years later. The Sandlers donated $1.3 billion shortly after they sold Golden West to Wachovia.

THE SACKLER FAMILY

Another low-profile influencer on the left is the Sackler family and their array of foundations. The Sacklers have a long family history which includes extensive philanthropy in the arts, university endowments for scientific and medical research, cultural heritage, famine relief and other more traditional philanthropic pursuits.

They also have their fingers in an extensive array of progressive political efforts. Mort Sackler made large contributions to the Clinton Foundation prior to Hillary's presidential run. Several other members of the Sackler family have supported Hillary with large checks over the years.[29]

The secretive family currently finds itself thrust into the spotlight and fighting off charges it started the opioid drug crisis which currently grips America.[30] Mort and Raymond Sackler made their fortune starting in the 1990s when the small pharmaceutical company called Purdue Pharma they inherited from their dad suddenly found itself making money hand over fist selling the newly FDA-approved OxyContin. A 2016 expose by the Washington Free Beacon revealed the extent to which the Sackler family immersed itself in Democratic Party politics, and noted significant questions existed whether Purdue Pharma fabricated the lab results that led to the approval of OxyContin.[31]

DRUMMOND PIKE

A child of the 1960s, Drummond Pike can reasonably be considered the pioneer of making the nonprofit sector a clearinghouse for donations to progressive causes. Pike started his activism career early, as an anti-Vietnam protester in college. Pike is widely heralded as the first person to incorporate donor-advised funds into issue advocacy and philanthropy.[32] Donor-advised funds allow the donor to make a contribution to a recognized nonprofit, thereby shielding their identity, while still retaining advisory privileges over how the money is spent. Pike did this via the Tides Foundation, which he co-founded in 1976 in San Francisco.[33] Pike also started the Tides Center, which became a distinct spinoff in 1996. Discover the Networks reports, "In 1979 Pike established the Tides Center to function as a legal firewall insulating the Tides Foundation from potential lawsuits filed by people whose livelihoods may have been harmed by Foundation-funded projects, and to serve as a fiscal sponsor for fledgling political advocacy groups."[34] Thus, Pike also pioneered the questionable concept of fiscal sponsorship mentioned in the 2014 Senate report regarding the Billionaire's Club. That report raised serious questions about the legality of sponsorship relationships, originally intended as temporary arrangements. The Senate Committee on Environment and Public Works found in its investigation some sponsorships had lasted as long as twenty-three years. The Tides Center still serves as a sort of donation clearinghouse, and the first step along what many consider a donation laundering chain.[35]

The Tides Foundation is no small enterprise. According to their 2016 audited financial statements posted on their website, the entire constellation of Tides organizations—consisting of a network of 501(c)(3) organizations, Tides Inc., and Tides Two Rivers Fund—brought in a combined $399,843,492 in total revenue that year.[36]

Among the programs supported by the Tides network is One PacificCoast Bank, which is now Beneficial State Bank—Kat Taylor's community banking enterprise.

JOHN ARNOLD

A billionaire who retired at thirty-eight, John Arnold and his wife, Laura, have spent their forties becoming active in philanthropy. John made his money as an energy trader for Enron before founding his own hedge fund and building his enormous personal fortune, estimated in 2018 around $3.3 billion.[37] The Arnolds actively insert themselves into causes, rejecting the notion that they can't run their own foundation. Some causes have merit, like their passionate support for charter schools and public pension reform. John has also become involved in evidence-based policy, and research integrity in scientific fields.

Some of their causes, however, push a far-left agenda aligned much more with Soros, Steyer, and Sandler. For instance, John

Arnold was a bundler for Barack Obama.[38] He also bankrolled a 2016 research project that advocated for a worldwide registry of wealth, 80 percent tax on income, worldwide wealth redistribution, and a global minimum income.[39] The main researcher, Frenchman Thomas Piketty, has earned the nickname "the Modern Marx." The research team's funding partners, as listed on their website:

- Center for Equitable Growth at UC Berkeley
- Institute for New Economic Thinking
- Laura and John Arnold Foundation
- NSF grant SES-1559014
- Russell Sage Foundation
- Sandler Foundation
- European Research Council under the European Union's Seventh Framework Programme[40]

The amounts of money passed back and forth and round and round in these philanthropic circles, with the sole purpose of funding environmental nonprofits to attack the economic engine of the United States, boggles the mind.

In the next chapter, we will examine who benefits from these arrangements, and who might be dumping resources into the effort.

CHAPTER 5

FALSE MORALITY
AND ILLICIT PARTNERS

*"It is essential to seek out enemy agents who have
come to conduct espionage against you and to
bribe them to serve you. Give them instructions
and care for them. Thus doubled agents are
recruited and used."*

—Sun Tzu

Herb Sandler's founding and funding of ProPublica comes
with a healthy measure of hypocrisy. It also reveals an all
too common desire among radical donors to subvert American
society, disavowing the greatness of America. Sometimes it can
lead them to forge alliances with foreign influencers.

Herb and Marion Sandler founded ProPublica in 2008,
at the very time when the economy had taken its nosedive

during the Great Recession. ProPublica's purpose, as stated on their website:[1]

> "ProPublica is an independent, nonprofit newsroom that produces investigative journalism with moral force. We dig deep into important issues, shining a light on abuses of power and betrayals of public trust—and we stick with those issues as long as it takes to hold power to account.
>
> "With a team of more than 75 dedicated journalists, ProPublica covers a range of topics including government and politics, business, criminal justice, the environment, education, health care, immigration, and technology. We focus on stories with the potential to spur real-world impact. Among other positive changes, our reporting has contributed to the passage of new laws; reversals of harmful policies and practices; and accountability for leaders at local, state and national levels."

Notice the one phrase? *Investigative journalism with "moral force."* What does that mean? It depends on whom you ask. For instance, if you ask the major liberal funders who back ProPublica, it likely means simply investigating Republicans. After all, Herb Sandler, as a major source of funding for MoveOn.org, has quite a history of ignoring or minimizing news items, like the cover-up of Bill Clinton's affair with Monica Lewinski, which precipitated MoveOn's creation in the first place. If those news items don't fit a particular objective, then they never show up at a news outlet run by someone with an agenda that would be derailed by such news.

That's what's known as selection bias—an editorial decision whether or not to report a particular item. Typically, selection bias doesn't show up on whatever fact-checking website one might reference to try to determine an outlet's bias.

In an opinion piece for the Daily Caller in 2017 in which he criticized the Pulitzer Committee for awarding ProPublica with a prize, Drew Johnson pointed out a clear case of bias in a report on charter schools:[2]

> "Enabling ProPublica and other such agenda-driven outlets—let alone rewarding them with a Pulitzer—gives them credibility they haven't earned. Consider the students and teachers at Sunshine High School, a charter school in Orlando, Florida.
>
> "Sunshine's student body is primarily made up of former high school dropouts and students referred to the school for academic intervention. A ProPublica reporter interviewed some of the students for a story on charter schools, a perennial annoyance of progressives. Unsurprisingly, the ProPublica report was a scathing article about the school's shortcomings. Administrators called out the reporter for missing the mark on the school's mission, as well as including quotes from minors without parental consent.
>
> "It's a sad day when left-wing advocacy bankrolled by liberal billionaires passes for disinterested journalism. Shame on the Pulitzer committee for rewarding ProPublica's bias."

Who besides Herb Sandler funds ProPublica? A litany of the largest foundations on the Left in America today: George Soros's Open Society Foundations, Obamacare advocate Atlantic Philanthropies, the John D. and Catherine T. MacArthur Foundation, the Ford Foundation, the Carnegie Foundation,

Pew Charitable Trusts, and other foundations with radical progressive agendas.[3]

Herb Sandler had another ulterior motive to want to create his own news outlet where he could control the output and the message, while hiding behind the mask of independence. Stung by the negative coverage and criticism the Sandlers received after selling Golden West Financial to Wachovia Bank, they had a strong motivation to find absolution—and maybe just a little measure of revenge. As chapter 4 noted, reporters and pundits repeatedly called Golden West "the Typhoid Mary of the subprime lending industry,"[4] and Sandler the most evil billionaire in the world. This probably didn't sit too well with the Sandlers. Certainly, their history of pursuing news outlets which mention these things and demanding retractions backs this up. In any event, possessing unlimited resources, a history of radical political patronage, and an axe to grind, Herb and Marion (before she passed in 2012) found their own forgiveness by providing the world with their vision of what investigative journalism should look like.

A similar scene is playing out with another major funder of progressive causes, the Sackler family and their various foundations. The press on both the Left and the Right have turned up the heat on the family company, Purdue Pharma, and the various lawsuits it faces over the production and marketing of OxyContin. The opioid addiction crisis has everyone's attention these days. According to the National Institute on Drug Abuse, overdose deaths for both synthetic opioids, like those prescribed as painkillers, and heroin have skyrocketed over the past ten years or so.[5] In 2010, deaths totaled fewer than five thousand for each nationwide, but today the number for synthetic opioids has jumped to twenty thousand. Heroin deaths have spiked to over fifteen thousand as of 2016. In this context, the family fortune and how the family doles it out have garnered extra scrutiny. As a big funding source in Democratic politics, the OxyContin money feels a little too icky for a lot of Democratic operatives. Never mind the fact the Sacklers have poured hundreds of millions in legitimate philanthropy dollars over the years into enormous art collections, university endowments, institutions of scientific research, and medical advancement. Various heirs have begun publicly feuding over which of the three brothers—Raymond, Richard, or Mort Sackler—deserves the most blame for whatever their part may be in the opioid crisis.[6] Absolution may elude this family for some time.

The examples of the Sandlers and the Sacklers show how sometimes the progressive billionaire donors realize their public image could use some rehabilitation, especially when journalists start digging into their political activity. It also provides a cautionary tale for those who wish to remain out of the spotlight.

As to the political activity itself, as previously mentioned, the Billionaire's Club understands, for the most part, that America doesn't agree with a lot of their agenda. Whether it be climate change, social justice, abortion on demand, or any number of controversial topics, the Left typically loses these debates in the public square. They know they have to tip the scales somehow in their favor. Luckily, they have a ready-made solution. They can always throw more money at the problem. That's sort of their stock in trade.

The radical Left and their wealthy liberal patrons fund an array of think tanks, foundations, supposedly unbiased polling outfits, and other entities that can quickly respond with messaging and talking points. These entities can counteract any attack by conservative forces or create a smokescreen behind which a radical public figure can hide. The two most familiar of these outlets are the Pew Charitable Trusts and the Southern Poverty Law Center (SPLC).

The media and the progressive Left treat the Southern Poverty Law Center as an authority on tracking hatred in America and fighting it in the courtroom. Founded in 1971, the original intent was to represent African-Americans in cases of discrimination, fighting poverty, and representing defendants in death row cases.[7] In 1979, the organization shifted toward something more lucrative: suing Ku Klux Klan chapters for monetary damages. In 1981, the SPLC began its Klanwatch project to monitor Klan activities. This effort eventually evolved into their Hatewatch effort that expanded the meaning of hate speech in America.

The SPLC took on an increasingly radical tone in the 1980s, with mixed results. The entire staff resigned in 1986 in protest of the more general attacks on conservatives. They also faced pressure as they became a more formidable fundraising operation. Nonetheless, the SPLC had built a bank of goodwill through the years as they defended African-Americans against white supremacists and Klansmen. One might even say they trade on the goodwill built up during the early years, but their current mission and organization bear little resemblance to those bygone days.[8]

Over the past couple of decades, the SPLC has evolved into more of a conservative-bashing organization which tries to conflate traditional American values with institutional racism. This can be quite useful for other radical organizations on the left that seek justification for their more extreme positions, such as America being inherently racist, the supposed ubiquity of institutionalized racism, and branding conservatives as filled with hate for groups they determine to be traditionally underrepresented.

One need look no further than the famous Hate Map they publish annually. When the Family Research Council finds themselves targeted by a crazed gunman intent on killing employees because they showed up on the SPLC Hate Map, you know your mission has crept away from its original intent. Indeed, the FBI has ceased citing SPLC as a credible source of information on potential criminal activity.[9]

Now, one thing the SPLC still does really well is fundraising. Fear mongering is good for the bottom line, apparently. A review of the SPLC by Philanthropy Roundtable said, in part: "Its two largest expenses are propaganda operations: creating its annual lists of 'haters' and 'extremists,' and running a big effort that pushes 'tolerance education' through more than 400,000 public-school teachers. And the single biggest effort undertaken by the SPLC? Fundraising. On the organization's 2015 IRS 990 form it declared $10 million of direct fundraising expenses, far more than it has ever spent on legal services."[10]

Think about that for a moment. It has never even approached $10 million in legal expenses, the original intent of the SPLC's founding, but annually spends that much just on fundraising.

It seems evident the SPLC's only remaining legitimate function is to provide intellectual cover for the policy positions of the most extreme leftist foundations which exist solely to brand conservative, traditional thought as hate speech. A compliant and sympathetic media are all too eager to perpetuate the long-dead myth of the SPLC as a legitimate, non-biased source of information on an ever-expanding definition of hate crimes.

ProPublica and Pew Charitable Trusts also provide intellectual cover for radical foundations to justify their extreme messaging. This then allows groups like Media Matters for America to come in and offer to work with media outlets and digital platforms to attempt to eliminate hate speech, report more efficiently on hate crimes, and stop the flow of fake news that has dominated the national conversation since Election Day 2016. In the confidential Plan to Kick Trump's Ass, distributed by David Brock to his donor gathering over Inauguration Weekend in 2017, he reveals he had already been in touch with Twitter and Facebook. He bragged Media Matters had access to the raw data from Twitter and Facebook, and Media Matters would work with the social media giants to root out and control right-wing views he labeled as fake news.

If the thought of David Brock having all of your raw data from Facebook and Twitter doesn't send shivers down your spine, you haven't been paying attention.

Not too long after the release of Brock's Plan to Kick Trump's Ass, reports of shadow banning began popping up more frequently. The concept is simple. Large conservative social media accounts accustomed to getting lots of interactions—likes, reposts, new followers, etc.—will see their traffic drop precipitously. Many have said their account all of a sudden won't be visible to their followers, even if the account is still active and not suspended.[11] In fact, Twitter engineers have admitted as much in undercover investigations and sting videos.[12]

Facebook and Twitter swear up and down they don't engage in this practice. Certainly, Brock's new partners in Silicon Valley have no reason to lie about it.

Except they have made numerous public statements about stopping the spread of fake news.[13] Facebook has begun tagging articles from certain outlets as questionable, and of course they famously limited everyone's personal news feed to include fewer posts from pages and more from actual friends. Twitter has banned several prominent conservatives for no apparent violation of their Terms of Service, with no explanation or appeals process.[14, 15]

In their ever-advancing effort to quash fake news, Google founded their First Draft news initiative. The following description appears on their website:[16]

ABOUT

First Draft—a project of the Shorenstein Center on Media, Politics and Public Policy at Harvard University's John F. Kennedy School of Government—uses research-based methods to fight mis- and disinformation online.

Additionally, it provides practical and ethical guidance in how to find, verify and publish content sourced from the social web.

Claire Wardle, Research Fellow at the Center, leads the work of First Draft under the auspices of the Shorenstein Center and its faculty director, Nicco Mele. Grants from the John S. and James L. Knight Foundation, Open Society Foundations and the Ford Foundation support our work.

HISTORY

First Draft grew out of a collaboration between nine founding organizations in June 2015 to raise awareness, perform research, and address challenges relating to trust and truth in media in the digital age. As one of the founding organizations, Google News Lab provided assistance to develop and maintain firstdraftnews.org, supported the creation of new content and coordinated the community of practice. In September 2016, First Draft began coordinating with a community of newsrooms, technology companies, human rights organizations and universities across the globe to help inform and scale its work, and to champion collaboration. In October 2017, First Draft moved to the John F. Kennedy School of Government at Harvard University, where it continues its work as a project of the Shorenstein Center on Media, Politics and Public Policy.

They go on to swear up and down the editorial decisions of the new outlet would never be influenced by their funding partnerships, because George Soros and the Open Society Foundations always work that way. Okay, that second part was an editorial, but not inaccurate.

All these efforts to stop fake news must be undertaken because clearly the Russian collusion and the fake news caused Hillary to lose to The Donald. That can be the only explanation. This is why Media Matters puts in so much effort to work with friendly reporters to ensure stories are properly propagated. It mirrors the Left's efforts to push public policy by seeding bureaucratic positions with fellow travelers, as in the case of John Beale at the EPA, or the World Resources Institute paying for a staffer in Washington Governor Jay Inslee's office. It also mirrors the Secretary of State Project from the early 2000s, and the current effort to get radical leftist attorneys general and district attorneys elected. If the Billionaire's Club can game the system to put their friends into the halls of government, then pushing their policy agendas through becomes that much easier. Why appeal to the voters when you can just have a bureaucrat write rules for you, or look the other way, or work with friendly attorneys on a sue-and-settle effort?

These donors and foundations operate by a different set of rules. When you have a pliable morality, the ends justify the means. More than anything else, that's the lesson of this book. Whatever it takes to push the agenda forward. Morality in this case means achieving those policy goals, no matter what.

"No matter what" could even include accepting influence and funding from foreign sources which have America's weakness in mind as their goal. Progressives want to believe the Russians stole the election after Donald Trump colluded with them during the campaign, but the evidence points in the opposite direction. As will be discussed, ample evidence exists to show that radical environmental and progressive protests and nonprofit groups have received significant funding from foreign sources, and it might have been occurring for a significant time. This obviously calls into question the motivations of the funders and what they hope to accomplish. It also raises those very uncomfortable questions for the nonprofit organizations, lobbying groups, and protest mobs themselves.

John Podesta, the former Chief of Staff to President Clinton and founder of the Center for American Progress, provides an excellent example of someone who should face a few uncomfortable questions. Like, hey, Mr. Podesta, in November 2017, your brother Tony abruptly closed up shop on the Podesta Group, a political lobbying firm that had been around and helping Democratic candidates and lobby interests for decades. Media reports indicate it was in connection with special prosecutor Robert Mueller's investigation into Russian collusion. Question: What's up with that?[17]

Despite his history as a successful fundraiser for Hillary Clinton's presidential campaign, having brought in over $900,000, Tony Podesta may end up in hot water over his connections to Paul Manafort and Rick Gates. Of course, brother John still actively involves himself in the Center for American Progress (CAP), funded by George Soros, Tom Steyer, and many others. Steyer still serves on CAP's board.

March 2018 marked a turning point in how America examines the foreign powers that influence our culture, amid a new enthusiasm for investigating how deep those influences go. While most of the radical Left maintained its focus on the dream of impeaching President Trump over collusion with the Russians during the election, the folks who do the big-boy reporting revealed connections of a far more signification kind. The month of March 2018 saw two reports released: one by *Foreign Policy* magazine detailing China's influence on American campuses, and one by the U.S. House of Representatives Committee on Science, Space, and Technology which went into great detail to describe Russia's efforts on social media to influence US domestic energy policy.

First, the Chinese influence. In the introduction, we briefly examined the far-left direct-action group By Any Means Necessary (BAMN) and their ties to the North American Man/Boy Love Association (NAMBLA). A professional riot group seems an odd pairing with a pro-pedophilia group, and when you throw in the Chinese government, well, buckle up.

Before we get to the 2018 *Foreign Policy* report, let's examine a dump of newly declassified FBI documents from 2017. Documents from investigations in the 1960s and 1970s show a clear connection between several radical students from the flower power era and promotion of the interests of the Chinese communist government.[18] These connections to Maoist influences in China may persist to this day. At the time, the radical organizations allied with the Black Panther Party, militant Hispanic organizations, and other extreme groups, and made statements favoring Viet Cong victory over the United States in the Vietnam War. This wouldn't move the needle too much today, fifty years later, except for the involvement of Floyd Huen. In the

1960s and 1970s, he was one of the most active radical protest-ers in the Red Guard Party, a pro-Mao communist group.[19]

Fast-forward to today. Huen has gotten very involved in progressive politics in California. His wife served as mayor of Oakland from 2011 to 2014. Huen at one time held the position of treasurer for Wellstone Action, a liberal foundation which works to carry on the vision of the progressive congressman from Minnesota. Wellstone Action is one of the main support-ers of BAMN, the Berkeley direct-action rioting group (with ties to NAMBLA), along with George Soros and the Open Society Foundations, which is a major funder of Wellstone. Funders include the Service Employees International Union, MoveOn. org, and others.[20]

So we have several foundations now which have direct influence—sometimes top leadership—from Maoist commu-nists, and they continue their struggle to this day by funding and supporting BAMN and other radical riot groups affiliated with Antifa, who also proclaim themselves pro-communist.

More than three hundred thirty thousand Chinese students attend college in the United States. The Chinese government funds and coordinates activities for dozens of branches of the Chinese Students and Scholars Association (CSSA) around America. In a March 2018 article, *Foreign Policy* magazine revealed the Chinese government often pays students to attend pro-China events, such as the rallies for Xi Jinping when he visits America.[21] *Foreign Policy* also describes a previous effort in which students were paid for their attendance: "And when then-President Hu Jintao visited Chicago in 2011 the University of Wisconsin-Madison CSSA bused in Chinese students, excited about a free trip to the city and a chance to glimpse the president. The association also surprised the students at the conclusion of the trip with a small cash payment. The CSSA president told students not to speak to the media about the money, according to one student who attended."[22]

The Chinese Embassy uses the app WeChat to coordinate with Chinese university students. As *FP* notes, "in the past few years, as Xi has strengthened the party's control over every aspect of Chinese society and sought to extend his power abroad, consular officials have markedly increased their efforts to exert ideological influence over students—leaving some CSSA members wary to speak out against what they see as unwanted government intrusion."[23]

The FBI has taken notice. Christopher Wray, director of the FBI, testified in front of the Senate Select Committee on Intelligence in February 2018. In this testimony, Wray said: "And I think the level of naïveté on the part of the academic sector about this creates its own issues. They're exploiting the very open research and development environment that we have, which we all revere, but they're taking advantage of it. So one of the things we're trying to do is view the China threat as not just a whole-of-government threat but a whole-of-society threat on their end, and I think it's going to take a whole-of-society response by us. So it's not just the intelligence community, but it's raising awareness within our academic sector, within our private sector, as part of the defense."[24]

Wray has subsequently stated in interviews that many industrial espionage investigations lead back to China.

Of course, though industrial espionage makes for a significant threat to America's industrial interests, perhaps more concern should be focused on China's attempts to negatively affect American culture and foment dissent.

Speaking of foreign powers fomenting dissent in America, it really is hard to know where to begin with Russia. The Russian government has their tentacles of influence in a lot of the institutions of the Left, from protest groups to nonprofits.

Let's start with the Clinton Foundation. The latest estimates indicate the Clinton Foundation received somewhere between $152 million and $173 million from private companies with close ties to Russia while Hillary was Secretary of State. In an article for *National Review* in March 2018, Deroy Murdock summarized the nature of these donations:[25]

- The Ex-Im Bank would welcome an application for financing from Rosavia to support its purchase of Boeing aircraft," Hillary said in Moscow on October 13, 2009. Three days later, according to the *Washington Post*, "Boeing formally submitted its bid for the Russian deal." Kremlin-owned Rostekhnologii decided on June 1, 2010, to buy up to 50 Boeing 737s for Aeroflot, Russia's national airline. Price: $3.7 billion. That August 17, Boeing gave the Clinton Foundation $900,000 to "help support the reconstruction of Haiti's public-education system" after a severe earthquake the previous January.

- Hillary pushed Skolkovo, "a high-tech corridor in Russia modeled after our own Silicon Valley," as she explained in Moscow in October 2009. Her State Department colleagues encouraged 22 top American venture capitalists to tour Skolkovo in May 2010. State convinced Cisco, Google, and Intel, among others, to open shop in Skolkovo. By 2012, 28 "Key Partners" from the U.S., Europe, and Russia supported this project. But the U.S. Army Foreign Military Studies Program warned in 2013: "Skolkovo is arguably an overt alternative to clandestine industrial espionage." Lucia Ziobro, a top FBI agent in Boston, explained in 2014: "The FBI believes the true motives of the Russian partners, who are often funded by their government, is to gain access to classified, sensitive, and emerging technology from the companies." An August 2016 Government Accountability Institute study titled From Russia with Money reported that 17 of Skolkovo's "Key Partners" plied Bill with speaking fees or gave the Clinton Foundation between $6.5 million and $23.5 million. (Some such donations, unfortunately, were reported in ranges, not precise sums.)

- Russia's State Atomic Energy Corporation, Rosatom, announced on June 8, 2010, a $1.3 billion bid for a majority stake in Canada's Uranium One. Its assets included 20 percent of American reserves of the main ingredient in atomic bombs. Hillary was one of nine federal-agency chiefs on the Committee on Foreign Investment in the United States, which evaluated this strategically sensitive proposal. As America's chief diplomat, Hillary could have sunk it. She didn't. Despite top Republican lawmakers' grave reservations, CFIUS approved Rosatom's offer and handed the Kremlin one fifth of U.S. uranium supplies. Before, during, and after CFIUS's review, Clinton Cash author Peter Schweizer calculates, "shareholders involved in this transaction had transferred approximately $145 million to the Clinton Foundation or its initiatives."

This sure looks like a Russian effort to collude with a presidential nominee from a major party.

It boggles the mind to consider the United States had a likely future president who worked for years behind the scenes to enrich her family with Russian influence and money, at the same time the Russians funneled money to environmental groups with the intent of undermining US domestic energy production while bolstering global Russian petroleum sales.

We now get to the March 2018 report by the House of Representatives Committee on Science, Space, and Technology, "Russian Attempts to Influence U.S. Domestic Energy Markets by Exploiting Social Media."[26] The report begins by noting the obvious: Russia has a significant interest in disrupting US energy production for reasons of global competition. "America's emergence as a global energy exporter presents a significant threat to Russian energy interests."

The reasons are obvious and should be met with resistance in America, not compliance and collusion. As the report says: "Such competition reduces the revenue and influence generated by Russian energy exports. This adversely affects the Kremlin's ability to leverage Eastern Europe's reliance on their energy and their ability to carry out their geopolitical agenda. The surge of American energy into the global marketplace heightens the Kremlin's desire to eliminate or mitigate the American energy threat and to do so by influencing social media users, American voters, and public officials."[27]

Let's pause for a moment and reflect on the notion that if one joins a protest movement which directly benefits a foreign power aligned against US interests, one could reasonably have to fend off accusations they are a willing dupe, at the very least, for Russia (or China), if not an outright collaborator. KGB defector Yuri Bezmenov, who ran many of the programs designed to subvert the free societies of the West, noted in a 1983 lecture that the KGB considered these types to be "useful idiots."[28] Of course, many radical protestors do so because they believe the US needs to be taken down in the global pecking order, so they're probably okay with that.

In a time when most experts expect US energy production to break records for several years to come, due entirely to our development of fracking technology,[29] Russia stands to lose both market share and influence over European states as more market competitors provide more choices.

The report goes on to detail the evidence showing Russia has supported environmental non-government organizations in Europe to protest and oppose shale gas exploration, to the tune of $95 million in material support. They do this to maintain European reliance on Russian petroleum and natural gas.

RT, formerly Russia Today, is a twenty-four-hour English language cable channel that gives the Russian view on the news. It has been accused of being little more than the propaganda arm of the Kremlin. Given all these attempts at influencing domestic energy policy, according to the House report, the Department of Justice in 2017 demanded RT register as a foreign agent under the Foreign Agents Registration Act (FARA). The House report summarizes, "FARA requires that agents representing the interests of foreign governments in any political or quasi-political capacity disclose public communications aimed at influencing American political debate or public policy."[30]

In 2016 and 2017, Russia ramped up its social media campaign against the Dakota Access Pipeline (DAPL), Keystone XL, climate change, the reliance of the United States on oil, and energy subsidies from the government. The House report says: "Beyond pipelines and infrastructure, a large portion of the Russian posts focused on framing America as a nation fixated on oil to the detriment of our political and social institutions. One post, for example, highlighted energy companies' profits and the energy-related 'subsidies' they receive and contrasted that with an apparent lack of subsidies for public school funding. Posts such as these use highly controversial issues to distort perceptions about the role energy companies play in American politics. Additionally, numerous posts advocated the complete abandonment of specific fuel sources, such as fossil fuels, by touting exaggerated claims about alternative energy sources. One such post, for example, touted the progress made by Iowa in its efforts toward clean energy. While Iowa does generate an increasing amount of energy from wind power, the post is false and an example of Russian efforts to mislead Americans regarding energy."[31]

The messaging used by the Russian social media accounts mirrors that of the most radical of the environmental groups in the United States. They didn't just post from the Left, however. The Russians often set up accounts which reflected a conservative viewpoint, using crude language to oppose environmentalism and stoke the emotions of social media users who favor petroleum production. This was an obvious, and in many cases successful, attempt to sow division among American voters. In a time of extreme political polarization, such divisions provided the Russians with ample opportunities to exploit wedges.[32]

The committee concluded the evidence clearly shows Russia attempted to influence public policy by roiling the waters on social media. They report social media companies have, so far, cooperated in identifying foreign influence. As they conclude, "Regardless of one's political or ideological views surrounding U.S. energy policy and climate change, the American people deserve to be free from foreign political interference."[33]

This is a very important front in battling foreign influence in American politics, but as we've examined, it is hardly the only one.

Remember the 2014 Senate report on the Billionaire's Club? They specifically targeted an environmental nonprofit called the Sea Change Foundation for scrutiny. Sea Change appears to have only three donors: Nat Simons, his wife, and a foreign corporation called Klein Ltd., based in Bermuda. The 2014 Senate report says: "The Billionaire's Club knowingly collaborates with questionable offshore funders to maximize support for the far-left environmental movement. The little information available on Sea Change is limited to a review of its IRS Form-990 for 2010 and 2011 as its 2012 form is not public, and a sparsely worded website—listing solely the logo and a three-sentence mission statement. Klein Ltd., an overseas company contributing tens of millions to organizations dedicated to abolishing the use of affordable fossil fuels through a U.S. private foundation is highly problematic. This is only compounded by the fact that it is deliberately and completely lacking in transparency—having no website and withholding its funders."

Klein Ltd. benefits from being located in Bermuda, which as a nation has no obligation to pay attention to IRS reporting requests, nor any other US reporting regulations. Of course, they categorically deny taking any Russian donations in their pass-through donations to environmental groups in the United States.[34] Given their refusal to provide detail and transparency, many have called for further congressional investigations into the operations of Klein Ltd. and Sea Change. After all, Sea Change has funded many of the biggest progressive nonprofits. The largest recipient of their grants is the radical Energy Foundation, another pass-through grantmaking group which funnels tens of millions into the environmental movement. The

Center for American Progress has also received large injections of cash from Sea Change.

America deserves to know which foreign powers attempt to influence public policy, their motivations, and their goals. We have a long way to go to achieve true transparency.

CHAPTER 6

THE ULTIMATE GOAL: A NON-CAPITALIST UTOPIA

"To declare the Cold War over, and declare democracy has won out over totalitarianism, is a measure of arrogance and wrong-headedness."

—ALEXANDER HAIG

Having established the how, we must now examine the why. Why do the elitist, leftist billionaires fund all these shady organizations, conduct all these hidden transactions, shield themselves from scrutiny—why do they do all of this to fundamentally transform our unique American way of life?

The EPA fraudster and compulsive liar John Beale, one of the stars of the chapter on Greenwashing, gave a glimpse into the motivations of the radical left when he gave a deposition to the prosecutors in his fraud case. He referenced a large project he and Robert Brenner wanted to tackle at the EPA:[1]

> "There were several phases of this project as we had outlined it...phase 1 of the project was for me to become very familiar and transversant with that literature. Phase 2 would have been out and interviewing academic experts, business experts, people in other countries that are doing things. *And then phase 3 would have been coming up with specific proposals that could be—could have been proposed either legislatively or things which could have been done administratively to kind of modify the DNA of the capitalist system. It's not a God-given system that was created once and never changes. It changes all the time."* (emphasis added)

Beale's idea to fundamentally change our economic system represents the prevailing views of most environmental radicals. He is not an outlier.[2] It has become the fashion to believe every societal ill was caused by the United States, and if we only had just a little more socialism, we could really fix things.

Indeed, a new book by two ecoradicals advocates for criminalization of dissenting thought. Dr. Peter Carver and Elizabeth Woodworth teamed up to write the book *Unprecedented Crime*, released in February 2018.[3] Carver founded the Climate Emergency Institute and has served as something called an "expert reviewer" for the International Panel on Climate Change. Woodworth is, paradoxically, an activist against increasing carbon dioxide emissions to limit man-made climate change, as well as an anti-nuclear activist. Together, Carver and Woodworth lay out a case in their book that anyone who disagrees with the orthodoxy on man-made climate change should be considered a criminal. The introduction states, in part: "*Unprecedented Crime* first lays out the culpability of governmental, political and religious bodies, corporations, and the media through their failure to report or act on the climate emergency. No emergency response has even been contemplated by wealthy high-emitting national governments. Extreme weather reporting never even hints at the need to address climate change. These willful crimes against life itself by negligent governments, oblivious media and an insouciant civil society are crimes that everyday citizens can nonetheless readily grasp – and then take to the streets and to the courts to protest on behalf of their children and grand-children."[4] In an interview, Carver explained the fossil fuel industry, the Republican Party, and those he labels as climate deniers, deliberately spread disinformation designed to deceive the public into believing there may exist some doubt about the truth of man-made global warming. To the extent such denial leads to the loss of human life, which he estimates to number in the millions in the future, he advocates using the criminal justice system to punish deniers.[5]

One review on the publisher's website put it into more blunt terms: "Criminal justice can contribute to addressing the climate crisis. A significant share of greenhouse gas emissions is associated with conduct amounting to violations of existing criminal law. Targeting climate change by enforcing criminal law can be extremely efficient. It can be done on the basis of existing laws, through existing institutions and with minimal additional cost. Peter Carver and Elizabeth Woodworth's book is a timely and important contribution to the debate regarding how criminal prosecutions, both at the national and international level, could be used to repress and deter climate damaging conduct at a large scale and on a lasting basis."

Astute readers at this juncture will note the ease with which this reviewer uses the word "repress," as if the concept of repression not only isn't foreign but tickles his fancy. They advocate for nothing less than using the criminal justice system as a tool to repress opposing thought. The constant drumbeat to criminalize dissent from leftist orthodoxy doesn't just occupy the fringes of the movement. It has taken hold in an ever-increasing swath of our society. The Bill of Rights gets in the way of a lot of efforts to change the United States, which necessitates actions to chip away at it, slowly and steadily. A handy rule of thumb: anytime someone wants to pass "common-sense" restrictions on natural individual rights, they have an ulterior motive. A narrative thread runs through the examples cited in this book: those ulterior motives get hidden in order to advance toward the goal unnoticed. Thus the importance of taking a look behind the curtain.

Take, for instance, the First Amendment. Most Americans who support the concept of freedom of speech would say some variation of, "I may disagree with what you say, but I would fight to defend your right to say it." On the other hand, many Americans might be swayed by the progressive argument that corporations aren't people, and might even engage in some sort of civilized debate on the limits to the rights to free speech.

The vast majority of Americans, however, have no idea that campaign finance reform and Net Neutrality have their origins in the same far-left attempt to fundamentally limit the First Amendment and criminalize certain forms of expression. If they did have such a notion, most Americans would recoil at such a blatant assault on individual liberty. The progressive-change agents driving the Left's agenda have become experts on testing these messages to make them seem like common-sense Americanism, instead of the subversive threats they actually are. They start with the easiest argument to make, like, "Corporations aren't people," and use the precedent to push for further and further encroachments on personal liberties.

Meet Robert McChesney, a professor at the University of Illinois at Urbana-Champaign. Like most Marxists, McChesney detests the concept of private property and the profit motive. He also believes, in order to make society more equitable, the government should be involved in regulating personal liberties. He utilizes the false premise of selling a scheme of control as making information more available to all. He co-founded Free Press, with both a 501(c)(3) and a 501(c)(4), that originally started the Media Reform Movement[6] McChesney described the reasons behind this movement in an article he wrote in 2014 for the *Monthly Review*, an independent socialist magazine, called, "Sharp Left Turn for the Media Reform Movement: Toward a Post-Capitalist Democracy."[7] He writes: "These are radical ideas, far outside the existing range of debate inside political circles or even the academy. Unless ideas along the lines of what follow get 'mainstreamed,' it will not just be the media reform movement but the broad political left that will be guaranteed irrelevance and failure."

Note well, this represents a broader theme for the radical Left; namely, they face enduring irrelevance without their ideas being granted artificial weight in the court of public opinion.

McChesney goes on to describe the movement itself: "The corruption of the media policymaking process was one of the founding concerns for Free Press and, if it is possible, the process has grown even more corrupt in the past decade. The U.S. political system has become what John Nichols and I characterize as a Dollarocracy. The vast majority of the population has no influence over core policies, regulations, taxation, or the budget, which are the province of large corporations and the very wealthy who dominate U.S. governance. Systemic corruption is the order of the day. The election system has been rendered largely ineffective as a means for citizens to engage in self-government. As former president Jimmy Carter said in 2013, the United States is no longer a 'functioning democracy,' even by the weak standards of its own history. This means the chances of winning media policy battles of any great consequence inside the beltway with the existing array of forces are all but non-existent."

Of course, what McChesney (and President Carter, for that matter) fails to understand is the inequitable system he criticizes was created, not by capitalism, but rather by progressive governmental intervention with regulations leading to unintended consequences.

Free Press now advocates for Net Neutrality and against media mergers. The two arms of Free Press receive lavish donations from the biggest and most radical donors on the Left[8] These donations usually flow to the 501(c)(3) first, so they can mask donor identities. In this sense, they commit the same hypocrisy shared by other progressive charities, by moving dark money around among their foundations to fight the influence in politics of...dark money.

Radicalism did not come recently to McChesney. He graduated from Evergreen State College in Olympia, Washington, which does not award letter grades for academic work. Evergreen State made news in 2017 for forcing a liberal, Bernie Sanders-supporting professor to resign. His crime? Expressing a view which conflicted with the Social Justice Warrior mob that enforces safe spaces and fights back against microaggressions on campus. In short, a tenured professor had his free speech denied by force by an angry student mob, for the offense of not toeing a line sufficiently to the left.[9] This is McChesney's academic background.

As a critic of capitalistic media, McChesney is a bit of a media whore himself, having written several books and innumerable articles, and conducted many, many interviews and lectures on the subject. He's gained a fair bit of notoriety, not to mention wealth, in doing so.[10] So we have a pretty good picture of his goals for the media as well as the American economy in general. He never misses an opportunity to criticize the free market as inadequate to match this societal challenge or that, and advocate for a command economy designed by elites like himself.

Conservative writer John Fund wrote a thorough break-down of McChesney and his billionaire patrons for the *Wall Street Journal* a few years back. In his column, "The Net Neutrality Coup," Fund draws a direct line between McChesney and the fight for Net Neutrality regulations, and the forces behind campaign finance reform.[11] As Fund notes, both campaigns propose to place wide restrictions on the First Amendment. He writes:

> "The net neutrality vision for government regulation of the Internet began with the work of Robert McChesney, a University of Illinois communications professor who founded the liberal lobby Free Press in 2002. Mr. McChesney's agenda? 'At the moment, the battle over network neutrality is not to completely eliminate the telephone and cable companies,' he told the website SocialistProject in 2009. 'But the ultimate goal is to get rid of the media capitalists in the phone and cable companies and to divest them from control.'
>
> "A year earlier, Mr. McChesney wrote in the Marxist journal *Monthly Review* that 'any serious effort to reform the media system would have to necessarily be part of a revolutionary program to overthrow the capitalist system itself.' Mr. McChesney told me in an interview that some of his comments have been 'taken out of context.' He acknowledged that he is a socialist and said he was 'hesitant to say I'm not a Marxist.'"

It remains unclear how McChesney can claim reluctance to the title of Marxist, as he routinely writes for socialist and communist outlets such as the *Monthly Review*, and in 2013 authored the book *Digital Disconnect: How Capitalism Is Turning the Internet Against Democracy.*

In any event, we will see here more of the same type of incest between activist foundations and federal bureaucrats that we saw in the EPA, governor's mansions, and other government agencies in earlier chapters. They do it for the same reasons, namely, to shield donors from scrutiny and to mask their true agenda. The Federal Communications Commission (FCC) employed several folks who formed a straight, unbroken line between Free Press and President Obama himself. The chief of the FCC under Obama was Julius Genachowski, a former law school chum of Obama's at Harvard. Genachowski hired Jen Howard as his press secretary. Howard previously worked in media relations at Free Press. On top of that, the FCC at the time also employed another former Free Press associate, Mark Lloyd, as their chief diversity officer.

The fight for Net Neutrality didn't occupy the back burner for the billionaires on the radical left. No, they made a massive investment in this movement. The Media Research Center reported, between 2000 and 2013, the most radical donors on the left poured $196 million into the campaign to regulate the internet.[12] These donations came from two major foundations on the progressive left we have previously examined: the Open Society Foundations, founded and funded by George Soros, and the Ford Foundation. Those two foundations plowed that money into an array of extreme groups on the left to engage in public pressure campaigns and lobbying. The Obama FCC passed Net Neutrality regulations in 2015, which essentially regulated the internet like a public utility under arcane rules written in the 1930s that had become obsolete, all in an effort to regulate an unfettered source of information, under the false premise of democratizing that information. Net Neutrality was the classic solution in search of a problem. Very few consumers experienced data slowdowns as a result of a lack of regulation, and in any event most internet service providers had implemented some sort of limited neutrality policy anyway. After its repeal late in 2017, consumers experienced no interruption or limitation in data access.[13]

When one realizes the unbroken chain between Net Neutrality and campaign finance reform, the goal becomes obvious. The radical progressive billionaires want nothing less than to regulate the natural rights inherent in each individual, as articulated in the United States Constitution. Most make it seem like they defend the First Amendment, when in fact it stands in the way of their agenda. Unregulated freedom cannot coexist with a command economy and society run by anti-capitalist elites.

The First Amendment reads, "Congress shall make no law respecting an establishment of religion, or prohibiting the free exercise thereof; or abridging the freedom of speech, or of the press; or the right of the people peaceably to assemble, and to petition the Government for a redress of grievances." Given the natural right of assembly and of free expression, most arguments for limiting information and speech evaporate.

Again, the agenda of the radical elites could not advance if most Americans realized the actual goals. Knowing this, progressives have become experts at creating messages that sound like common sense. In his column, Fund cites a 2004 talk by Sean Tregalia at the University of Southern California. You can still find this talk on YouTube under the title *Fake Mass Movement*.[14] In it, Tregalia reveals how, when he worked at Pew Charitable Trusts, they created the deliberate illusion of a mass movement to get money out of politics altogether. They made the illusion feel even bigger by creating imaginary support out of whole cloth that business groups, academic groups, ethnic groups, religious institutions, and others supported this movement, and that a groundswell was building among grassroots activists. Tregalia reveals the campaign finance reform movement had almost zero basis in a grassroots uprising of voters. "The idea was to create an impression that a mass movement was afoot," says Tregalia. "If Congress thought this was a Pew effort, it'd be worthless." Fund notes, "A study by the Political Money Line, a nonpartisan website dealing with issues of campaign funding, found that of the $140 million spent to directly promote campaign finance reform in the last decade, $123 million came from eight liberal foundations."

Fund then goes on to describe how, after the McCain-Feingold Act passed, these progressive foundations and their radical donors shifted focus to the "media reform movement." That was about the same time McChesney co-founded Free Press and started bringing in donations previously earmarked for the campaign finance movement. They wanted to create a sort of Fairness Doctrine for the internet. The Federal Communications Commission created the Fairness Doctrine in the 1940s to require radio and television stations to present controversial issues, and further, to present both sides of an issue. Otherwise, the FCC said, stations were to remain neutral in matters of public policy and politics. The FCC removed the Fairness Doctrine in 1987, after reasonable people noted its blatant unconstitutionality—in effect, the Fairness Doctrine required certain types of expression, and forbade others.

Ever since that FCC ruling, the Left has wanted to reinstitute the Fairness Doctrine, and they want to extend it from over-the-air broadcast stations to the internet as well. They make the argument that talk radio, which overwhelmingly skews to the right, should be forced to present all sides. They fail to acknowledge or allow for consumer choice, of course. The abject failure of progressive talk radio to provide a counterbalance to conservative talk radio should give the Left all the example they need that their ideas fail to resonate with most Americans. Radical progressives take this example and, instead of learning from it, and moderating their views to connect with more voters, decide that expression should be limited, their agenda must move forward even more forcefully, and their true motives must be hidden so as not to turn off voters and their representatives until it's too late.

This effort to rig federal agencies represents only one front in the war to regulate liberty. The recent March for Our Lives, precipitated by the horribly tragic shooting at Marjory Stoneman Douglas High School in Parkland, Florida, displays every sign of this. In a move straight out of the playbooks of the radical billionaires, it took about fourteen seconds for the biggest progressive organizations out there to co-opt the student movement in favor of gun reform.

Okay, fourteen seconds is a bit of an exaggeration—but not much of one. Several students who survived the Parkland shooting became media celebrities and activists virtually overnight. This handful of students began demonstrating for gun control, holding rallies and marches, and conducting endless interviews for an eager media. Soon, however, the biggest players on the left, along with radical Hollywood celebrities, took the movement over completely. It became obvious the moment the protests expanded nationwide, as a couple of high school juniors wouldn't have the resources or experience to apply for rally permits in cities across the nation, create merchandise to sell, set up websites and groups nationwide, or apply for tax-exempt status with the IRS. In fact, they state on their website, "Your contribution will benefit March for Our Lives Action Fund, a 501(c)(4) social welfare organization."[15] Of course, March for Our Lives Action Fund has no obligation to reveal its donors.

Luckily, most of the donors had no hesitance over bragging about their support of March for Our Lives. Turns out, most of this movement has been propagated by familiar organizations—the Michael-Bloomberg-funded Everytown for Gun Safety, EMILY's List, the Women's March, Moms Demand Action for Gun Sense in America, the Joyce Foundation, and many others. This doesn't even include the Hollywood elites who have pledged enormous donations, such as the celebrities who pledged $500,000: George and Amal Clooney, Oprah Winfrey, Jeffrey Katzenberg, Steven Spielberg, and clothier

Gucci. John Legend and Chrissy Teigen offered twenty-five thousand dollars, while business leaders Eli Broad and Marc Benioff donated one million dollars each.[16] Both the dating app Bumble and the Miami Dolphins gave one hundred thousand dollars, and many others did not disclose the amounts of their pledges. Jared Kushner's brother Josh also gave $50,000. The New England Patriots allowed kids from Parkland to use the team plane to go to the DC march, and ride hailing app Lyft gave anyone a free ride to and from any rally listed on the March for Our Lives website.

Let's examine Everytown for Gun Safety for a moment. On the March for Our Lives website, in the FAQs, the following two entries appear:

CAN I MAKE TAX-DEDUCTIBLE CONTRIBUTIONS TO THE ACTION FUND?

No. March for Our Lives Action Fund is tax-exempt under section 501(c)(4) of the Internal Revenue Code. Unlike section 501(c)(3) charitable organizations which have restrictions on their lobbying activities, section 501(c)(4) organizations are permitted to conduct unlimited lobbying for federal tax purposes. This form of entity gives the students maximum flexibility to conduct high-impact legislative advocacy during the Day of Action and beyond. The trade-off is that contributions are not tax-deductible.

IS THERE A SECTION 501(C)(3) MARCH FOR OUR LIVES ORGANIZATION?

You can make tax-deductible contributions to support the March For Our Lives movement and student-led activism by supporting the March For Our Lives Initiative at Everytown for Gun Safety Support Fund. Checks should be made payable to:

March For Our Lives—Everytown Support Fund
Everytown for Gun Safety Support Fund
PO Box 3886
New York, NY 10163[17]

Now March for Our Lives will not file IRS 990 forms until 2019, so we don't have an advance look at their financial arrangements. We can surmise a few things, however. Because March for Our Lives has stated on its website that it operates as a 501(c)(4), they likely have not worked out a sponsorship arrangement with Everytown to rent that group's nonprofit status, like other nonprofits examined earlier. It is not a stretch to surmise, however, that the Everytown for Gun Safety Support Fund, where donors can make a tax-deductible donation to the 501(c)(3), will be sending grants to the March for Our Lives 501(c)(4). Indeed, we've seen this with the endless cycle of back-and-forth grantmaking among different progressive organizations.

These massive donations have the same goal. The donors, foundations, and celebrities want to create the illusion that this student-led grassroots movement represents common-sense and popular views on gun control. Knowing gun control does not resonate with most Americans, they must hide the influence of big money while driving toward the inevitable goal of severely restricting the Second Amendment—or reversing it altogether.

A lot of money has already poured in—some from some unexpected sources but the vast majority coming from the usual suspects.

Speaking of money pouring in to undermine a basic American freedom, the ability to purchase inexpensive energy and power for our homes and our transportation has come under increasing assault in recent years. In 2015, Rep. Raul Grijalva, a Democratic congressman from Arizona, sent letters to seven universities where professors taught climate science.[18] The letter questioned the impartiality of each of the seven climate scientists and demanded each university disclose potential conflicts of interest. Those supposed conflicts of interest? Whether the universities in question received financial support from energy companies.

Later that same year, after prodding by liberal US Sen. Sheldon Whitehouse of Rhode Island, twenty climate scientists sent a letter to President Obama and Attorney General Loretta Lynch demanding they use the Racketeer Influenced and Corrupt Organizations (RICO) Act to investigate and prosecute energy companies for their denial of man-made global warming.[19] Lawmakers originally designed RICO to take down the mafia and other organized crime outfits.

The Heartland Institute, a free-market think tank in Chicago which bills itself as the world's most prominent think tank promoting skepticism about man-made climate change, pointed out the danger of using such statutes to suppress debate and free speech. In a 2016 article, Heartland quoted E. Calvin Beisner, spokesman for the Cornwall Alliance for the Stewardship of

Creation, who said, "Just by contemplating such a prosecution, the government has undermined the foundations of Western Civilization."

"The threat of such actions to free speech, free inquiry, and the free and vigorous debate that are central to the whole Western understanding of liberty, of intellectual health, and of science is real and ominous," Beisner said. "America's Founding Fathers would reject this idea instantly."[20]

Meanwhile, another group has decided to use the legal system to repress dissenting views. This time, a group of kids has decided to sue any governmental agency they can even remotely connect to climate change on the grounds they deny children the right a future with a stable climate. Under the misguided notion that the government and the judicial system grant rights, the nonprofit Our Children's Trust sues governments, as they say on their website, to secure "the legal right to a safe climate and a healthy atmosphere for all present and future generations."[21] With a budget of almost $400,000 in 2016, according to their IRS Form 990s, the money has to come from somewhere to pay their immense legal bills. Their ongoing list of sustained donations includes The Rockefeller Brothers Fund, which has contributed several hundred thousand dollars since 2011, when the fund was seeded with a total of $1.1 million in donations and grants.

So we see these actions, and the question remains: What goals are these organizations and donors trying to achieve? We need to look no further than George Soros, who told us the goals himself, in a 1997 article in *The Atlantic* magazine.[22] Whereas one might write off billionaires like Tom Steyer and Michael Bloomberg as socialist control freaks, Soros has a grander vision of a global government, one that is based in rejection of Nazism and communism, but has now evolved to include the rejection of laissez-faire capitalism. He introduces his philosophy by first quoting Hegel and laying out a case that, now that communism has fallen apart, capitalism represents the greatest threat to democracy. "Although I have made a fortune in the financial markets," Soros writes: "I now fear that the untrammeled intensification of laissez-faire capitalism and the spread of market values into all areas of life is endangering our open and democratic society. The main enemy of the open society, I believe, is no longer the communist but the capitalist threat." Under an open society, Soros proposes to remove existing social and political institutions, the notion of national sovereignty, and the free market system—which he describes as creating social inequities—and replacing them with what he describes as more cooperative social structures. Soros contends, "an open society may also be threatened from the opposite direction—from excessive individualism. Too much competition and too little cooperation can cause intolerable inequities and instability. Insofar as there is a dominant belief in our society today, it is a belief in the magic of the marketplace. The doctrine of laissez-faire capitalism holds that the common good is best served by the uninhibited pursuit of self-interest. Unless it is tempered by the recognition of a common interest that ought to take precedence over particular interests, our present system—which, however imperfect, qualifies as an open society—is liable to break down."

Soros bases his arguments on false premises. He believes free market capitalism creates a sort of religious fervor in individuals, similar to Marxist dogma, which can lead humanity to seeking an absolute truth. Importantly, he rejects the concept of absolute truth outright. He takes the concept of human fallibility and misapplies it to truly free markets.

Soros's philanthropic efforts have accelerated since he first became involved in philanthropy in 1979. His contributions to his Open Society Institute since that time exceed $25 billion, and as discussed earlier, that money has seeded some of the most subversive and anti-capitalist efforts in America.

Soros can protest all he wants that he seeks more transparency, more openness, more cooperation, and less influence from dictators such as Vladimir Putin and Xi Jinping. There must be a reason, however, Russian and Chinese interests have funneled massive donations into the same causes and foundations and protests that Soros himself has supported.

Whether or not the other members of the Billionaire's Club share the open society views with Soros, the means to the end remain the same. It's all about correcting societal inequities via the means of wealth redistribution. "By taking the conditions of supply and demand as given and declaring government intervention the ultimate evil," Soros continued, "laissez-faire ideology has effectively banished income or wealth redistribution. I can agree that all attempts at redistribution interfere with the efficiency of the market, but it does not follow that no attempt should be made. The laissez-faire argument relies on the same tacit appeal to perfection as does communism. It claims that if redistribution causes inefficiencies and distortions, the problems can be solved by eliminating redistribution—just as the Communists claimed that the duplication involved in competition is wasteful, and therefore we should have a centrally planned economy."

So, let us review. The goals of the Billionaire's Club include creating a more perfect state. They believe they can eliminate inequity if only they gain control of the levers of governance. From limiting speech and expression, to limiting the sources from which an individual consumer can get their news, to limiting the very personal liberty to defend oneself, the fact remains that individual liberty itself stops the agenda. For all of these billionaires and their goal of reshaping the world to their ideal image, the American free market system, with the ultimate expression of individual liberty codified for the first time in human history in the Bill of Rights, presents a massive impediment to their vision of a more cooperative, more regulated, more redistributionist society.

CONCLUSION

*"The devil's finest trick is to persuade you that he
does not exist."*

—CHARLES BAUDELAIRE

M any people believe the money spent on politics so per-
verts the American electoral system as to render it
obsolete, broken, and in need of replacement. It seems utterly
impossible to know who influences the politicians, how that
influence leads to the production of public policy, and who
benefits most when bills get signed into law. Most Americans
have an instinctual reliance on the axiom Follow the Money,
but they don't know where to look. Most Americans also have a
healthy distrust of the politicians who craft the laws. Too many
Americans, therefore, simply give up on the task of unraveling
these webs of influence. Of course, this only favors those who
would hide their influence and suppress the turnout of actual
informed voters on Election Day.

The progressive foundations and nonprofits on the radical left have become masters at demonizing their enemies. David Brock pitches his vast array of interconnected nonprofits as a direct attempt to fight back against such conservative institutions as the Heritage Foundation and Media Research Center. Brock alleges the nonprofits on the Right have unlimited resources with which to wage war on social justice, climate justice, progressive causes, and all the other fringe ideas that constitute the modern radical Left. In that pitch, he deliberately flips the script. Demonizing the Koch Brothers provides cover for the exact same strategy used on the left. As Chris Horner of the Competitive Enterprise Institute and E&E Legal Institute said, as quoted earlier, "Just substitute the phrase, 'So it's okay if the Koch Foundation pays the salary of the Wyoming energy advisor?'" The levels of double standards applied by the Left, nakedly, brazenly, and deliberately, become just so much background noise—especially when a compliant media agrees to cooperate with the message.

Demonization of the Right allows them to create a sort of hypocrisy feedback loop. "The Right does this," they'll say, "so we must do it too in order to compete, and we do it for a more noble cause, so we use dark money to get dark money out of elections because of the Evil Koch Brothers." Or something like that.

So we end up in a sort of an arms race, where foundations on the right and the left continually feel pressure to keep up and not lose ground to the other side. Many of the examples cited in this book clearly show the Left fights dirty. George Soros has seeded the Open Society Foundations with $18 billion in a succession plan to keep them running long after he's gone. Tom Steyer continues to ramp up his efforts and his donations, still occupying the top spot on the list of individual political donors. Bill Gates and Warren Buffett continue to add billionaires to the Giving Pledge list, currently well over 150 active members. Pledges from that effort run into the hundreds of billions of dollars, with a large proportion of those donations going to causes on the left. Michael Bloomberg continues to meddle in the affairs of states far away from where he lives. The Pew Foundation continues to be a reliable source of public opinion data, despite their massive efforts to advance the progressive agenda. The Southern Poverty Law Center gets a seat at the table, no matter how skewed their definition of hate groups. Facebook founder Mark Zuckerberg has billions to play with and has already funded the Silicon Valley Community Fund with large donations of Facebook stock. Foundations like the Hewlett Foundation, the Packard Foundation, the Ford Foundation, the Rockefeller Foundation, the Sandlers, the Sacklers, and an endless array of others still control hundreds of millions in philanthropic assets. When you add all that up, it comes to tens of billions per year spent promoting and advancing a progressive agenda in the halls of American government. It's difficult to conceive of the full scope of the money spent and influence exerted for progressive causes.

Some of these donors like to see their names in the news, so they go all out to get in front of a story they think will reflect well on them. Look no further than elitist billionaire Michael

Bloomberg's efforts to raise sin taxes in states across the nation, and his efforts on gun control. Bloomberg thinks he knows better than the average American consumer what they should and shouldn't put into their bodies, and has made it one of his life's missions to get every state and municipality in the union to raise taxes on soda. Having no conception of what it's like to be poor, he has no awareness of how disproportionately these taxes affect people of lower income. He simply sees a supposed public health crisis, in this case childhood obesity, and thinks, as an elite, he can posit a better solution than anybody else. Using the mechanism of government to punish consumers not only doesn't sway him, he seems to enjoy it. Just one problem: evidence shows that unless the tax is enormous, it won't significantly affect behavior. On top of that, if a city imposes a soda tax, evidence strongly indicates many, if not most, consumers will just go to the next town over to pay less for the soda they will consume anyway. A soda tax, therefore, is nothing more than a revenue grab. Bloomberg, however, just keeps on chugging away at making himself a hero of public health. Bloomberg also either doesn't understand, or doesn't care, that gun control doesn't actually work. He puts himself out as the public face of this supposed public health issue, as well.

Tom Steyer similarly loves the spotlight. His wife, Kat Taylor, prefers to let him be the star of the show, while her banking enterprise continues to profit from the favorable government regulations passed by politicians and bureaucrats supported by her husband. Meanwhile, Steyer himself profits handsomely when his agenda finds a friendly agency and becomes law. He augments his email list and donations to his nonprofits by staying in the news, pushing for impeachment and winking away speculation he might run for office someday.

The worst thing an elitist can do is to presuppose their idea is better than anyone else's and fail to test their hypothesis. This leads to bad public policy with terrible outcomes for most, while the elites continue to profit.

This model of influence and money got its start over forty years ago, in San Francisco, with a handful of the more forward-thinking flower children who decided they really wanted to change the world. The Tides Foundation and its associated Tides Center continue to accept huge sums of donations, as well as government grants, which they can then funnel into radical organizations. Founded by Drummond Pike, Tides demonstrated the full potential of donor-directed funds. They showed the world nonprofits can advance a donor's agenda without that donor fearing their identity and intentions would see the light of day.

Many donors don't wish to endure public scrutiny. The Tides Foundation showed progressive foundations how they could guarantee them a measure of secrecy when the donor makes a gift. The progressive donors and their foundations can and do intentionally hide their true goals.

One might reasonably conclude these efforts to shield donor identity amount to money laundering. Again, if it looks like a duck, quacks like a duck, and swims on a giant pile of money like a duck, it must at least be a member of the waterfowl family. The grantmaking process back and forth among charities, foundations, PACs, and super PACs creates a veil that can be difficult to pierce. As we discovered when uncovering the interrelationships with the David Brock groups, the FEC and the IRS only have one-way systems of checking. There is no way to get the full picture of who donates, where the money gets funneled, and who actually buys the influence exerted on politicians and bureaucrats.

This type of foundational layering that takes advantage of donor-advised funding presents another advantage to donors. They maintain layers of separation which create what Discover the Networks called a firewall against liability, lawsuits, and other legal actions undertaken by those whose life or work might be negatively impacted by the activities of foundations sponsored by Tides. Donors thus stay above the fray, and above reproach.

Speaking of David Brock's interrelated groups, the expense-sharing agreements among separate entities, including office rental, shared employees, and a common paymaster, create an extra layer of opaqueness that blocks ever more sunlight. Current laws and regulations around campaign finance allow for some of these layers of opaqueness, so long as the groups provide the proper reporting to state and federal agencies charged with keeping track of the details.

Hopefully, we will find out soon whether Brock's sloppy reports amount to the violations they appear to be.

When examining the secrecy around these liberal billionaires, their progressive foundations, and their radical agenda to change America, one thing becomes obvious: they use every means at their disposal, legal or not, to shield themselves from scrutiny. This is because they must. If American voters realized the true nature of this progressive agenda, they would reject it outright. Example after example in this book shows this to be true.

So when violent riots show up on our nightly news, or a new protest group springs up out of nowhere, America seems continually caught off guard, while the mainstream media play up the panic and the chaos for ratings. When the unintended (or, often, intended) consequences of environmental regulations impact an industry, we wonder how it happened and who caused it. When a teachers strike becomes larger than the number of teachers in the district, we wonder where all these people came from. We sometimes have difficulty connecting the dots between minimum-wage protesters, anti-conservative demonstrations, illegal immigrant rallies, and other demonstrations. How do these things all seem to happen simultaneously? Why can we not rely on our elected officials to do the right thing? How is it district attorneys, attorneys general, or judges in some states seem to side more often with non-citizens than with citizens? We often have no idea who pulls the strings, but we suspect these politicians and bureaucrats don't work alone. The protesters who would fade into oblivion five minutes after the rally ends suddenly find themselves with an enduring spotlight which magnifies their image and their message.

Those who pull the strings hide their agendas because they have to hide them. They know that much of the progressive agenda, radical environmentalism, redistribution, oppressive taxation, and governmental interference in markets won't move the needle for a large number of voters. Every once in a while, they let their guard down and even admit they know how unpopular the agenda is, as the former Pew employee did at USC in 2004. For the most part, however, they keep it bottled up. They know the really radical stuff they push is anathema to the American experiment. So they stay behind the curtain as much as they can.

When that curtain gets pulled back, when the sunlight hits the dark money, when the activities of the radicals hit the mainstream, it doesn't just derail them. They react like Nosferatu on a garlic farm in California. They have to answer questions. They must endure scrutiny. They might even face some hard questions about the popularity or effectiveness of their policies.

On the rare occasion when that happens, it's usually not the fault of the media. So many members of the media align politically with the progressive billionaires. Many of them went from radical foundations directly into the news business, where they should conduct actual journalism and hold their friends accountable. Too often, they'd rather just not worry about that, preferring instead to freak out about a tweet storm by Donald Trump, make wild allegations about Russian collusion while ignoring a certain failed presidential candidate's connections, or conduct investigative journalism on some sort of philanthropic venture by a conservative donor.

That's just fine with liberal news editors, bureaucrats at state and federal agencies, progressive lawmakers, and those who organize the street protests. When an unbroken line exists between these areas, they can work better in concert when the agenda does not get exposed to the light of day.

So, what's the solution?

First, we must recognize how big the network of influencers is, and how much money and power they wield. We must also recognize they will never willingly give up that money and power.

Once we establish widespread recognition of the massive scope of the issue, the question turns to the appropriate counterbalance. An appropriate set of solutions to problems created by excessive regulations would not include corrective regulations. As a rule, relying on the government to regulate itself makes little sense, with unintended consequences almost always in the offing. Besides, rarely can you expect government to do anything efficiently. That government is best which governs least, said Henry David Thoreau.

Trying to rewrite campaign finance law and IRS code is a fool's errand, anyway. We saw that in McCain-Feingold, much of which is slowly but surely being completely dismantled in Supreme Court case after Supreme Court case. The latest example, *Citizens United*, shows clearly that limiting expression does not comport with the First Amendment.

We can start by enforcing the laws we have on the books now. As Andrew Kerr noted when he described his FEC complaint against Media Matters, currently no cooperation exists between the FEC and the IRS. "Ultimately, I'd like to see out of this that the FEC consider rules about cost sharing," said Kerr. "There's no oversight between these organizations that both the

IRS and the FEC look at. Hopefully this is a wakeup call for them. You've got this gray area that nobody's looking at. There could be some serious, serious abuses taking place that are going completely over your head."

Just like so much of what goes on today, like the immigration issue, Kerr goes on to say we don't need new laws, just better enforcement. "We don't need reform of the law. The law is very clear. You give something of value to a PAC, it needs to be reported. There's just a lack of oversight. Reform the organizations that are supposed to be overseeing our electoral process, and are not doing their job properly. It's kind of an insult that somebody like me had to go through all this. The FEC should be doing this."

Certainly, the pipe dream of the Left to repeal the *Citizens United* decision via a constitutional amendment will never happen. Even if it somehow passed, it would not solve the problems progressives claim it would. Money has been in American politics since at least 1800, when Aaron Burr organized enough donations to help propel Thomas Jefferson into office. Indeed, it goes back further than that, and the Framers of the Constitution recognized that placing limits on political cash would violate the document they produced.

Ultimately, the most powerful solution consists of millions of informed voters. Agencies receiving requests under the Freedom of Information Act should process them with haste. Public records should never be hidden. Documents should never endure the slow walk from a recalcitrant public agency or unelected bureaucrat protecting a fiefdom. Investigative journalists should remain free to go wherever the money and paper trail lead them. Indeed, we have lots of room for growth in investigative journalism and legal pressure to make agencies more accountable to the people. Citizens should have access to any information they wish to review. Should public records reveal criminal conspiracies, prosecutors should aggressively pursue charges regardless of party alignment.

Thomas Jefferson had a favorite Latin phrase, *Malo periculosam, libertatem quam quietam servitutem*. It means, "I prefer the tumult of freedom to the peace of slavery." That uniquely American tumult includes the best political movements money can buy, along with the best accountability an informed citizenry can apply. It's up to each individual to take the personal responsibility to gain knowledge of the issues, and also of the influencers. Discover the agendas. Hold them accountable, especially when they work deliberately to subvert the Constitution.

It is the hope this book has given the reader a glimpse behind the curtain. It would be foolhardy to attempt an exhaustive catalogue of all the radical organizations and all the progressive funders who are pushing this subversive agenda. Nevertheless, by citing prominent examples and their not so well known agendas, the aspiration is that readers will be empowered to make informed decisions, peel back curtains on their own, and understand the who, the how, and the why behind the radical agendas the elites intend for you.

THE FOUNDATIONS

There exists an endless array of political nonprofits, foundations, PACs, and super PACs which spend astronomical sums to influence American society and push it inexorably to the left. This appendix could not possibly catalogue all of them. Instead, it's intended as a reference to some of the biggest foundations around, and some of their most prominent activities. Combined, these organizations spend billions of dollars annually in various attempts to reach Americans and change their minds. They employ veritable armies of well-compensated operatives to achieve these goals. These foundations connect directly back to the wealthy founders discussed throughout the book. In many cases, they were founded by billionaires who still actively manage them. In a few instances, the foundations were long ago founded by stalwarts of capitalism who wished to see their vast wealth used in perpetuity to improve the human condition. The heirs of these great visionaries, however, don't share the same values. As we will see, many of these entities have taken on the polar opposite philosophy of their founder.

Open Society Foundations/ Open Society Institute

A comprehensive listing of the endless progressive causes and campaigns funded by Soros's OSF and OSI would be impossible. The following representative sampling, while in no way comprehensive, will provide a good idea of the philosophical bent of the movements they support (courtesy of Discover the Networks).[1]

- The Center for Economic and Policy Research asserts that "the welfare state has softened the impact" of "the worst excesses and irrationalities of a market system" and its "injustices."

- Democracy for America operates an academy that has taught more than ten thousand recruits nationwide how to "focus, network, and train grassroots activists in the skills and strategies to take back our country."

- People for the American Way, co-founded by television producer Norman Lear to oppose the allegedly growing influence of the "religious Right," seeks "to cultivate new generations of leaders and activists" who will promote "progressive values."

- The Ruckus Society promotes "nonviolent direct action against unjust institutions and policies." (Note: remember this term, "direct action," when examining the activities of Antifa and other protest groups. The members of Ruckus went on to join Antifa and to found By Any Means Necessary, two of the most active and violent protest groups since Election Day 2016.)

- The Ella Baker Center for Human Rights was founded by the revolutionary communist Van Jones. This anti-poverty organization claims that "decades of disinvestment in our cities," coupled with America's allegedly imperishable racism, have "led to despair and homelessness."

- The Brennan Center for Justice aims to "fully restore voting rights following criminal conviction"—significant because research shows that ex-felons are far likelier to vote for Democratic political candidates than for Republicans.

- Free Press is a "media reform" organization co-founded by Robert McChesney, who calls for "a revolutionary program to overthrow the capitalist system" and to "rebuil[d] the entire society on socialist principles."

- Media Matters for America: For a number of years, the Open Society Foundations gave indirect funding—filtering their grants first through other Soros-backed operations—to this "progressive research and information center" which "monitor[s]" and "correct[s]" conservative misinformation in the U.S. media." In October 2010, Soros announced that he would soon donate one million dollars directly to Media Matters. (This is David Brock's empire that currently faces FEC complaints.)

- The American Constitution Society for Law and Policy seeks to indoctrinate young law students to view the Constitution as an evolving or "living" document, and to reject "conservative buzzwords such as 'originalism' and 'strict construction.'" (Note: Supreme Court Justice Ruth Bader Ginsberg has spoken at events hosted by this group.)

- *Sojourners* characterizes wealth redistribution as the fulfillment of a biblical mandate. Jim Wallis, the founder of this evangelical Christian ministry, has expressed his hope that "more Christians will come to view the world through Marxist eyes."

The Open Society Foundations has also given hundreds of millions in grants to the Tides Foundation over a period of a couple of decades. Gara LaMarche, who now serves as president of the donor organization Democracy Alliance, previously served as vice president of the Open Society Institute. With well over $14 billion in donations and grants over almost forty years, the list could go on forever, but this representative sample should provide a good feel for what George Soros wants to see happen to America. Remember, he claims to have started out as a committed anti-communist, before coming to the view that capitalism represented the greatest risk to his vision of open societies[2]. The Democracy Alliance, as we'll see, has its finger-prints all over Black Lives Matter and Antifa.

Tides Foundation

Similar to the Soros groups, the vast network of grantors and grantees engaged by the Tides Foundation far exceeds an honest attempt to catalogue. Again, a small sampling will give a broad understanding:[3]

- The Liberty Hill Foundation, a relatively small foundation in comparison to Tides or OSI, was founded by four wealthy heirs in 1976. They set out to make phi-lanthropy more active, as opposed to what they saw as maintaining the status quo. Win McCormack was one co-founder who, in later life, settled in Portland, Oregon. A successful publisher, prior to joining Liberty Hill he co-founded *Mother Jones* magazine. McCor-mack in 2016 purchased *The New Republic* magazine. He authored the book *You Don't Know Me: A Citizen's Guide to Republican Family Values* in 2008. In 2014, McCormack was singled out as a prominent Oregon resident who knew about Oregon's governor, Neil Goldshcmidt, and his relationship in the 1970s with his fourteen-year-old babysitter. McCormack, a supposed investigative journalist, helped keep the secret for decades, well past the statute of limitations, until the then-forty-three-year old woman died of a drug overdose.[4] McCormack has given hundreds of thousands in personal donations to David Brock's American 21st Century Bridge PAC, an outfit which tracks and records prominent Republicans.

· National Resources Defense Council (NRDC), with current annual revenues north of $150 million, has produced some of the most costly environmental hoaxes in US history, including the 1989 scare about apple pesticide Alar. Among the more radical of NRDC's positions, environmental justice plays a prominent role. As Discover the Networks says: "By NRDC's telling: 'Communities of color, which are often poor, are routinely targeted to host facilities that have negative environmental impacts—say, a landfill, dirty industrial plant or truck depot.' The Council pledges to fight this insidious 'environmental racism.'"

· The Rockefeller Fund regularly receives grants from the Tides Foundation, while also oddly awarding grants back to the Tides groups. The Rockefeller Fund currently has over $4 billion in assets, and awards almost $200 million in grants every year to progressive causes. This doesn't even count the separate Rockefeller Brothers Foundation and the Rockefeller Family Foundation.

- The Black Lives Matter (BLM) movement received significant support from Tides in the form of grants to People Organized to Win Employment Rights (POWER).[5] Tides also funded the Ruckus Society, which partnered directly with BLM. Other foundations which contributed to groups supporting BLM include Soros's Open Society Foundations, the Rockefeller Fund, the Ford Foundation, and others which were organized and encouraged at the Spring Conference of the Democracy Alliance in 2015. The Tides Foundation, of course, is one of the most generous members of the DA.

- People for the Ethical Treatment of Animals (PETA) describes itself as the largest animal rights organization in the world and supports the international terrorist group Animal Liberation Front.

- Directly following the election of Donald Trump, the Tides Foundation started Indivisible, the previously mentioned organization which modeled itself on the American Tea Party Movement and vows to resist the Trump administration. Their funding was framed as a mystery by public radio, but the About page at Indivisible.org says:

"How to Donate: Individuals interested in making tax deductible contributions online are encouraged to donate to the Indivisible Fund, a project of the Tides Foundation, a 501(c)(3) organization."[6]

The Tides Foundation has also received massive grants from the Ford Foundation, the Hewlett Foundation, the Packard Foundation, the Open Society Institute/Foundation, Pew Charitable Trusts, the Bill and Melinda Gates Foundation, and many others. A significant portion of the annual revenue of the Tides Center consists of government grants.[7]

In addition, according to the 2014 Senate report "The Chain of Environmental Command," the various entities continually pass grants back and forth. "Between 2010 and 2012," the report states: "Tides Foundation gave over $10 million to Tides Center, and Tides Center gave over $39 million to Tides Foundation. It is unclear what purpose the transfer of funds between these two organizations serves, other than obscuring the money trail. Tides Center is a fiscal sponsor to over 200 groups, which are subject to Tides Center's oversight and direction in important aspects that include forming a governing board, managing payroll, and monitoring risk."[8]

The Sackler Foundations

A foundation was established in the names of each of the main family members involved in Purdue Pharma: father Mort, who purchased Purdue in 1952, and brothers Raymond, Richard, and Arthur. All have involved themselves to various degrees in funding Democratic Party initiatives, including the Clinton Foundation, Hillary's campaigns for senate and president, and the DNC.

The William and Flora Hewlett Foundation

This is one of the biggest, baddest, most flush-with-cash foundations on the left, and barely anyone has heard of them. The William and Flora Hewlett Foundation, started in 1966, awards grants in amounts that match the annual budgets of other foundations. One could say William Hewlett was Bill Gates before Bill Gates was born. Upon his death in 2001, Hewlett bequeathed five billion dollars to his foundation to fund it in perpetuity.[9] Hewlett gets involved in education and the arts, but their main impact happens in the environmental grantmaking world. Their total revenue in 2016 topped out over $600 million. As of 2016, Hewlett's assets exceeded $9 billion, and they awarded over $425 million in grants.[10]

The Hewlett Foundation operates much like the Tides or the Energy Foundation. Utilizing the model pioneered by Tides in the 1970s, Hewlett takes donor-directed grants which then get redirected out to grantees of the donor's choice. Utilizing this donor-directed model under a 501(c)(3) structure, donors get a tax write-off for their donation, tell the foundation where to send the money, and remain completely anonymous. Hewlett is the eight hundred-pound gorilla in the room in the radical progressive nonprofit world.

The Ford Foundation

Like the Rockefeller Foundation below, which was created from wealth gained in the oil industry, the Ford Foundation was created by another great capitalist of the twentieth century but continues to send obscene amounts of funding to radical groups that wish to undermine capitalism. As of 2016, Ford claimed assets of over $12 billion.[11] In 2014, they claimed income of $658 million,[12] but in 2016 that dipped to just under $218 million. They consistently award over $500 million in grants each year. The conservative views of Henry Ford made way for a much more radical direction in the 1960s. As Discover the Networks notes: "[T]he Ford Foundation, particularly during the Nixon years, came to see itself as a government-in-exile, an engine for social transformation. [New President McGeorge] Bundy transformed the Foundation into a leading sponsor of left-wing causes such as the expansion of the welfare state, nuclear disarmament, environmental advocacy, and the creation of 'civil rights' interest groups that emphasized ethnic identity and ethnic power, or 'multiculturalism,' over integration and assimilation into the American culture. Ford gave as much as $300 million per year throughout the 1960s to support such causes."[13]

$300 million per year would be a lot today. In 1966, it was an astronomical sum. The last Ford family member to serve on the foundation board, Henry's grandson, resigned in disgust at the leftward turn of the organization in 1976. In his resignation letter, Henry Ford II said: "The Foundation exists and thrives on the fruits of our economic system. The dividends of competitive enterprise make it all possible. A significant portion of the abundance created by U.S. business enables the foundation and like institutions to carry on their work. In effect, the foundation is a creature of capitalism—a statement that, I'm sure, would be shocking to many people in the field of philanthropy. It is hard to discern recognition of this fact in anything the foundation does. It is even more difficult to find an understanding of this in many of the institutions, particularly the universities, that are the recipients of the foundation's grant programs."[14]

The hijacking of a foundation created by one of the great capitalists in American history by radical leftists, who continue to fund the most extreme progressive causes, remains a shock to this day.

The Rockefeller Foundation

Originally founded in 1913, the Rockefeller Foundation currently has assets valued at just over $4 billion and awarded $400 million in grants in 2015.[15] The Rockefeller Family Foundation and the Rockefeller Brothers Foundation also play significant roles in funding radical nonprofits, but they are no match for dad's original foundation.

The Sea Change Foundation

The Sea Change Foundation got its start in 2005 as a nonprofit explicitly dedicated to addressing climate change, through leveraged philanthropy. While it awards a significant amount in grants every year ($42 million in 2014), its numbers don't put it at the top of the philanthropy mountain. It's more worth noting the business dealings of Sea Change than noting the grant totals themselves.

Sea Change showed up in the Billionaire's Club Senate report from 2014, when alarm bells went off about possible foreign sources of funding. Sea Change is the third-largest donor to the Energy Foundation, detailed below, and acts as a donor-directed nonprofit which allows donors to state where they want their money to go. They also give heavily to Sierra Club and the Center for American Progress.[16] Sea Change was co-founded in 1982 by James Henry Simons, and is now run by his son Nathaniel "Nat" Simons. Klein Ltd. is the largest donor by far, and they just so happen to be located in Bermuda. In fact, *The Billionaire's Club* report paints a pretty blatant picture of possible corruption at Sea Change. "Sea Change's IRS Form 990 also shows that in addition to funding by the Simons, the only other source of its contributions derives from a Bermuda-based company called Klein Ltd."[17] They further note: "It appears that Klein exists on paper only, as it does not have an internet presence, and was set up for the sole purpose of funneling anonymous donations to Sea Change. In 2010, Klein contributed $13 million to Sea Change, amounting to 49% of all contributions to Sea Change that year, and in 2011 Klein contributed $10 million to Sea Change, amounting to 33% of all contributions to Sea Change. Bermuda offers Klein government guaranteed anonymity for the sources of their donations. As a practical matter, an overseas company contributing tens of millions to organizations dedicated to abolishing the use of affordable fossil fuels is highly problematic."

As we will examine later, overseas interference in many aspects of the progressive activist Left requires much more scrutiny than it currently receives.

Environmental Grantmakers Association

The Rockefeller Foundation, the Ford Foundation, and Sea Change are all members of the Environmental Grantmakers Association (EGA). The EGA is another pass-through nonprofit which screens donor identities while allowing them to make donor-directed contributions. The 2014 Senate report gave a handy chart showing the largest donors to EGA:[18]

Top 10 EGA Donors to Environmental Causes in 2011

Foundation	Total Dollar sigis Awarded	No. of Grants
Gordon and Betty Moore Foundation	$134,438,760	251
David and Lucile Packard Foundation	$121,016,258	207.
Walton Family Foundation, Inc.	$76,218,045	105
William and Flora Hewlett Foundation	$53,439,469	115
Rockefeller Foundation	$43,809,793	117
Sea Change Foundation	$43,149,911	42
Richard King Mellon Foundation	$29,080,000	41
Robertson Foundation	$28,507,000	16
John D. and Catherine T. MacArthur Foundation	$24,204,500	60
Ford Foundation	$23,922,840	108
Total:	$577,786,576	1,034

This chart just shows the top ten. The website LeftExposed. org calculates EGA members, about 200 in all, gave over $1 billion to qualified environmental nonprofits—just in 2012.[19] This number represented 38 percent of all environmental grantmaking philanthropy that year. As we will examine later, overseas interference in many aspects of the progressive activist Left requires much more scrutiny than it currently receives.

Energy Foundation

LeftExposed.org reveals the Energy Foundation received 611 grants from 124 foundations from 1997 to 2015, totaling $534,010,014.[20] They list the top fifteen donor foundations as:

- WILLIAM & FLORA HEWLETT FOUNDATION, $149,028,172

- DAVID AND LUCILE PACKARD FOUNDATION, $70,664,800

- SEA CHANGE FOUNDATION, $64,818,332

- MCKNIGHT FOUNDATION, $52,191,300

- JOHN D & CATHERINE T MACARTHUR FOUNDATION, $22,066,748

- DORIS DUKE CHARITABLE FOUNDATION, $21,140,000

- MERTZ GILMORE FOUNDATION, $18,735,000

- ROCKEFELLER FOUNDATION, $5,595,000

- PEW CHARITABLE TRUSTS, $4,947,600 .

- GOOGLE FOUNDATION, $4,695,000

- TOMKAT CHARITABLE TRUST, (Tom Steyer) $4,150,000

- THE OAK FOUNDATION USA, $1,434,997

- BLOOMBERG FAMILY FOUNDATION INC, $750,000

- TIDES FOUNDATION, $355,000

- ROCKEFELLER BROTHERS FUND INC, $250,000

The report describes the Energy Foundation by saying: "The Energy Foundation is an unconventional 'pass-through' financing organization created by a consortium of left-leaning foundations acting as 'partners.' It was incorporated in San Francisco, California on October 15, 1990 as a 501(c)(3) exempt private foundation on behalf of three progressive agenda-focused foundations, the John D. and Catherine T. MacArthur Foundation, the Pew Charitable Trusts and the Rockefeller Foundation." In structure and function, it operates very similarly to Tides, DA, and other donor-directed pass-through grantmaking operations which serve to shield donors from scrutiny. During that same 1997–2015 period when it received $534 million in grants, it doled out $1.2 billion in grants to various environmental groups.

Public Sector Unions

Of course, no discussion of political influence on the radical left could aspire to completeness without delving into the operations of labor unions, and in particular, the public sector unions. For decades, labor has represented a stronghold for funding of liberal candidates and causes. The Service Employees International Union (SEIU) is a founding member of the Democracy Alliance, and granted it $295,000 in 2015.[21] In 2016, they spent just shy of $25 million on federal elections, mostly on independent expenditure campaigns (super PACs), and almost all on liberal causes. This doesn't include their work at the state level, which was a much higher amount. Along with funding the DA, the SEIU provides large amounts of funding for liberal groups such as Center for American Progress, Tides, Demos, Planned Parenthood, and the League of Conservation Voters. Of course, the SEIU has a never-ending funding stream in the form of member dues, which makes them the most reliable source of support for radical causes.

So what you end up with is a multibillion-dollar political funding machine which relies on subterfuge, forced union dues, foreign influence, money originally derived from sources that the radical progressives despise, and possible criminal activity to cover it all up and avoid reporting requirements.

ENDNOTES

Introduction

1   https://web.archive.org/web/20180520222843/http://www.wweek.
com/portland/article-1553-all-quiet-in-little-beirut.html

2   https://web.archive.org/web/20170901050347/http://www.cnn.com
/2017/08/18/us/unmasking-antifa-anti-fascists-hard-left/index.html

3   https://web.archive.org/web/20170830102247/
http://thehill.com/blogs/pundits-blog/
civil-rights/348389-opinion-antifa-threatens-to-turn-america-into-an

4   https://web.archive.org/web/20170426041405/http://www.wweek.
com/news/2017/04/25/street-fight-fears-lead-to-parade-cancelation/

5   https://web.archive.org/web/20170430004650/http://www.oregonlive.
com:80/rosefest/index.ssf/2017/04/organizers_cancel_82nd_avenue.
html

6   https://web.archive.org/web/20170429001940/https://dailycaller.
com/2017/04/28/documents-tie-berkeley-riot-organizers-to-pro-pedo-
philia-group-nambla/

7   https://web.archive.org/web/20161114155438/http://www.oregonlive.
com:80/portland/index.ssf/2016/11/pearl_district_ne_portland_wak.
html

8   https://web.archive.org/web/20170521114451/
http://www.dailywire.com:80/news/10834/video-anti-trump-rioters
-bash-pregnant-womans-car-chase-stephens

9   https://web.archive.org/web/20180406022043/
     https://www.frontpagemag.com/fpm/269649/
     whos-really-behind-march-our-lives-daniel-greenfield

10   https://web.archive.org/web/*/https://
     www.plannedparenthoodaction.org/blog/
     highlights-the-march-for-our-lives-and-the-fight-to-end-gun-violence

11   https://web.archive.org/web/20170628180959/https://nypost.
     com/2017/06/28/when-your-job-pays-you-to-protest/

12   https://web.archive.org/web/20170506230135/https://www.sfchronicle.
     com/business/article/Bay-Area-demonstrators-may-be-paid-to-pro-
     test-by-11125584.php

13   https://web.archive.org/web/20171215133655/http://www.cracked.
     com/personal-experiences-2476-i-know-paid-protesters-are-real-
     because-im-one-them.html

14   https://web.archive.org/web/20180504050651/https://psmag.com/
     news/in-defense-of-paid-protesters

15   https://web.archive.org/web/20131101161049/http://www.nydailynews.
     com/news/national/new-york-teamsters-local-237-bus-support-
     union-protestors-wisconsin-article-1.135548

Chapter 1

1   https://web.archive.org/web/20171102163622/http://money.cnn.
     com/2016/10/12/media/donald-trump-polls/index.html

2   https://web.archive.org/web/20180306113015/https://www.esquire.
     com/news-politics/a13266971/election-2016-behind-the-scenes/

3   https://web.archive.org/web/20180501025331/http://www.discover-
     thenetworks.org/printgroupProfile.asp?grpid=6709

4   https://web.archive.org/web/20171129090018/https://www.thedaily-
     beast.com/can-anyone-ever-truly-trust-david-brock

5   https://web.archive.org/web/20180120232059/http://time.
     com/4641901/trump-inauguration-david-brock/

6   Ibid.

7   Ibid.

8   https://web.archive.org/web/20170920202524/http://www.oregonlive.
    com:80/portland/index.ssf/2017/03/homeland_security_calls_port-
    land_trump_riot_domestic_terrorist_violence.html

9   https://web.archive.org/web/20180502182417/https://www.politico.
    com/story/2017/09/01/antifa-charlottesville-violence-fbi-242235

10 http://archive.li/SKoZ9

11 https://web.archive.org/web/20180520224121/https://www.nationalre-
    view.com/2017/08/antifa-berkeley-protest-turns-violent-again/

12 https://web.archive.org/web/20180518170525/https://www.theatlantic.
    com/magazine/archive/2017/09/the-rise-of-the-violent-left/534192/

13 Ibid.

14 https://web.archive.org/web/20171114161510/
    http://dailycaller.com:80/2017/08/20/
    pee-filled-projectiles-a-recurring-weapon-of-choice-for-anti-fascists/

15 https://web.archive.org/web/20180326012329/http://www.oregonlive.
    com/portland/index.ssf/2016/11/pearl_district_ne_portland_wak.html

16 https://web.archive.org/web/20180510235348/https://www.theatlantic.
    com/magazine/archive/2017/09/the-rise-of-the-violent-left/534192/

17 https://web.archive.org/web/20171004185450/https://www.indivisible.
    org/about-us/

18 https://web.archive.org/web/20180512222722/https://www.influence-
    watch.org/non-profit/the-indivisible-project-indivisible/

19 https://web.archive.org/web/20170503063816/https://ballotpedia.org/
    Democracy_Alliance

20 https://web.archive.org/web/20180421063916/http://freebeacon.com/
    politics/resistance-royalty-pelosi-soros-headline-lefts-biggest-dark-
    money-conference/

21 https://web.archive.org/web/20180516224804/https://www.politico.
    com/story/2016/11/democrats-soros-trump-231313

22 https://web.archive.org/web/20180507174809/https://www.politico.
    com/story/2016/11/david-brock-donald-trump-donor-network-231588

23 https://web.archive.org/web/20180517054119/http://freebeacon.com/politics/david-brock-memo-attack-trump/

24 https://web.archive.org/web/20180509174553/https://www.scribd.com/document/337535680/Full-David-Brock-Confidential-Memo-On-Fighting-Trump

25 Ibid.

26 https://web.archive.org/web/20171017091225/http://rightwingnews.com/democrats/girl-scouts-caught-using-far-left-soros-funded-website-to-indoctrinate-girls/

27 https://web.archive.org/web/20171215003230/https://en.wikipedia.org/wiki/Citizens_for_Responsibility_and_Ethics_in_Washington

28 https://web.archive.org/web/20180430191344/http://www.thecitizensaudit.com/2016/09/19/money-laundering-david-brock/

29 https://web.archive.org/web/20180509174553/https://www.scribd.com/document/337535680/Full-David-Brock-Confidential-Memo-On-Fighting-Trump

30 https://web.archive.org/web/20171117004459/http://www.pewresearch.org:80/topics/polling/

31 https://web.archive.org/web/20180520071432/http://www.pewresearch.org/about/

32 https://web.archive.org/web/20180520224942/https://capitalresearch.org/article/pew-and-the-gang-ride-again-citizens-free-speech-still-in-danger/

Chapter 2

1 https://web.archive.org/web/20180202121622/https://www.thecitizensaudit.com/author/andrewthecitizensaudit-com/

2 https://web.archive.org/web/20180501032629/https://www.nytimes.com/2015/02/06/us/in-invisible-world-of-political-donor-advisers-a-highly-visible-player.html

3 https://web.archive.org/web/20180219062314/http://www.thecitizensaudit.com/2017/10/09/american-bridge-21st-century-cost-sharing-explainer/

4   https://web.archive.org/web/20180425235714/
    https://www.scribd.com/document/369806983/
    True-the-Vote-v-IRS-Consent-Order-Jan-21-2018

5   https://web.archive.org/web/20180510022038/https://www.nytimes.
    com/2015/05/03/us/politics/fec-cant-curb-2016-election-abuse-com-
    mission-chief-says.html

6   https://web.archive.org/web/20180302115703/https://www.
    idealist.org/en/consultant/5f6f5f492f0844cf9661f27ac2dba
    b8b-bonner-group-inc-washington

7   https://web.archive.org/web/20180520225530/https://www.buzzfeed.
    com/rubycramer/how-a-clinton-insider-fight-turned-public?utm_
    term=.myLJAvYRo#.wi1W4V67a

8   https://web.archive.org/web/20180506062433/http://www.afpnet.org/
    Ethics/EthicsArticleDetail.cfm?ItemNumber=734

9   https://web.archive.org/web/20180430191344/http://www.thecitizen-
    saudit.com/2016/09/19/money-laundering-david-brock/

10 https://web.archive.org/web/20180429090001/https://mybusiness.
    dc.gov/

11 https://web.archive.org/web/20180430191344/http://www.thecitizen-
    saudit.com/2016/09/19/money-laundering-david-brock/

12 Ibid.

13 https://web.archive.org/web/20180121033228/https://www.zerohedge.
    com/news/2016-09-20/money-laundering-scheme-exposed-14-pro-
    clinton-super-pacs-non-profits-implicated

14 https://web.archive.org/web/20180219062314/
    http://www.thecitizensaudit.com/2017/10/09/
    american-bridge-21st-century-cost-sharing-explainer/

15 Ibid.

16 Ibid.

17 https://web.archive.org/web/20180518193423/https://sunlightfounda-
    tion.com/about/

18 https://web.archive.org/web/20180518154516/
    https://sunlightfoundation.com/2016/02/10/
    shifting-super-pac-cash-makes-it-even-harder-to-follow-the-money/

19 https://web.archive.org/web/20180520225149/http://www.
    thecitizensaudit.com/wp-content/uploads/2017/10/AB-Foundation-
    Itemized-Offsets-2011-June-2013.jpg

20 https://web.archive.org/web/20180520225149/http://www.
    thecitizensaudit.com/wp-content/uploads/2017/10/AB-foundation-
    Itemized-Offsets-July-2013-December-2015.jpg

21 https://web.archive.org/web/20180219062314/
    http://www.thecitizensaudit.com/2017/10/09/
    american-bridge-21st-century-cost-sharing-explainer/

22 https://web.archive.org/web/20171113002913/http://www.thecitizen-
    saudit.com:80/2017/10/10/the-citizens-audit-files-fec-complaint

23 https://web.archive.org/web/20170728192459/https://transition.fec.
    gov/info/conference_materials/2013/candidateterminologymarch13.
    pdf

24 https://web.archive.org/web/20171224014845/https://www.merriam-
    webster.com/dictionary/launder

Chapter 3

1   https://web.archive.org/web/20171022141600/http://eelegal.org/
    wp-content/uploads/2015/08/EE-Legal-111d-etc-Steyer-et-al-Report-
    8-24-15-Final.pdf

2   https://web.archive.org/web/20180512172330/http://freebeacon.com/
    issues/tom-steyers-deep-ties-to-oregon-corruption-scandal/

3   https://web.archive.org/web/20161223051206/http://www.
    npr.org/sections/thetwo-way/2015/02/13/386074092/
    amid-influence-peddling-scandal-oregon-governor-resigns/

4   https://web.archive.org/web/20171022141600/http://eelegal.org/
    wp-content/uploads/2015/08/EE-Legal-111d-etc-Steyer-et-al-Report-
    8-24-15-Final.pdf

5   Ibid.

6   https://web.archive.org/web/20170307144356/http://www.wweek.
    com/portland/blog-32782-kitzhaber-hired-ally-who-arranged-cylvia-
    hayes-fellowship-making-him-highest-paid-aide.html

7   Ibid.

8   http://www.guidestar.org/ViewPdf.aspx?PdfSource=0&ein=27-1762207

9   https://web.archive.org/web/20140825072840/http://cleaneconomy-
    center.org/advisors

10 https://web.archive.org/web/20180512172330/http://freebeacon.com/
    issues/tom-steyers-deep-ties-to-oregon-corruption-scandal/

11 https://web.archive.org/web/20180520231105/
    http://www.koin.com/news/
    hayes-faces-100000-plus-in-fines-for-ethics-violations/918062234

12 https://web.archive.org/web/20180116033741/http://www.oregonlive.
    com/politics/index.ssf/2018/01/oregon_ethics_commission_cylvi.html

13 https://web.archive.org/web/20180404233714/http://p3hubamericas.
    partnershipsevents.com/speakers/speaker/aGyTyrPW

14 https://web.archive.org/web/20171022141600/http://eelegal.org/
    wp-content/uploads/2015/08/EE-Legal-111d-etc-Steyer-et-al-Report-
    8-24-15-Final.pdf

15 https://web.archive.org/web/20180430135518/https://www.wsj.com/
    articles/climate-of-unaccountability-1515717585

16 https://web.archive.org/web/20180520231344/https://projects.pro-
    publica.org/nonprofits/organizations/521257057

17 https://web.archive.org/web/20171022141600/http://eelegal.org/
    wp-content/uploads/2015/08/EE-Legal-111d-etc-Steyer-et-al-Report-
    8-24-15-Final.pdf

18 https://web.archive.org/web/20180520231344/https://projects.pro-
    publica.org/nonprofits/organizations/521257057

19 https://web.archive.org/web/20170716094721/http://www.wri.org/
    sites/default/files/uploads/FY2016_Regular_Audit_Report.pdf

20 https://web.archive.org/web/20170801122549/https://www.usclima-
    tealliance.org/

21 https://web.archive.org/web/20180131013521/https://www.usclimateal-liance.org/alliance-principles/

22 https://web.archive.org/web/20150913140935/https://www.epw.senate.gov/public/index.cfm/press-releases-republican?ID=53280DCB-9F2C-2E3A-7092-10CF6D8D08DF

23 https://web.archive.org/web/20180321171302/http://leftexposed.org/wp-content/uploads/2016/01/2014-Senate-Billionaire-Club-Report.pdf

24 Ibid., pp i-ii

25 Ibid., p iv

26 Ibid., p 5

27 Ibid., p 7

28 https://web.archive.org/web/20180403234316/https://350.org/about/

29 https://web.archive.org/web/20180321171302/http://leftexposed.org/wp-content/uploads/2016/01/2014-Senate-Billionaire-Club-Report.pdf, p 8

30 Ibid., p 7

31 https://web.archive.org/web/20170919195958/https://ega.org/about/faq

32 https://web.archive.org/web/20170724055105/http://www.rbf.org:80/grantmaking/grant-opportunities

33 https://web.archive.org/web/20180321171302/http://leftexposed.org/wp-content/uploads/2016/01/2014-Senate-Billionaire-Club-Report.pdf, p 5

34 Ibid.

35 Ibid.

36 Ibid.

37 Ibid., p vi

38 https://web.archive.org/web/20151016134946/https://www.epw.senate.gov/public/_cache/files/2d30f39e-2fde-4b37-8810-32fa21b6e6bd/epa-playbookunveiled.pdf

39 Ibid., p i

40 Ibid., p iv

41 Ibid., p ii

42 Ibid., p 26

43 https://web.archive.org/web/20171112055501/https://searchfinancialse-curity.techtarget.com/definition/Dodd-Frank-Act

44 https://web.archive.org/web/20180521155625/https://www.weeklystandard.com/ronald-l-rubin/donald-trump-evicted-elizabeth-warren-from-the-consumer-financial-protection-bureau

45 https://web.archive.org/web/20180427084807/https://slate.com/business/2017/12/the-cfpb-under-mick-mulvaney-has-a-new-mission-ending-burdensome-regulations.html

46 http://archive.is/M0tRE

47 Ibid.

48 https://web.archive.org/web/20180521162757/https://cei.org/blog/consumer-financial-protection-bureau-slush-fund?utm_source=twitter&utm_medium=social&utm_campaign=comms

Chapter 4

1 https://web.archive.org/web/20180520070125/https://givingpledge.org/

2 https://web.archive.org/web/20180502104637/https://www.politico.com/story/2014/04/democrats-democracy-alliance-liberal-donors-105972

3 https://web.archive.org/web/20171215092049/https://www.scribd.com/document/364798053/Soros-Democracy-Alliance-Leak-pdf

4 http://archive.li/https://democracyalliance.org/about/

5 https://web.archive.org/web/20180124200310/http://freebeacon.com/politics/david-brock-memo-attack-trump/

6 https://web.archive.org/web/20180321171302/http://leftexposed.org/wp-content/uploads/2016/01/2014-Senate-Billionaire-Club-Report.pdf

7 https://web.archive.org/web/20180520232900/https://www.influence-watch.org/non-profit/nextgen-climate-action/

8 https://web.archive.org/web/20180331102920/https://www.opense-crets.org/overview/topindivs.php?cycle=2016&view=fc

9 Ibid.

10 https://web.archive.org/web/20171109004941/http://eelegal.org/wp-content/uploads/2016/07/Steyer-Report-7-21-2016.pdf

11 https://web.archive.org/web/20180301215732/https://www.usnews.com/news/the-report/articles/2018-02-16/tom-steyer-the-billionaire-who-could

12 https://web.archive.org/web/20171229135839/https://www.newyorker.com/magazine/2013/09/16/the-president-and-the-pipeline

13 https://web.archive.org/web/20140425143722/https://freebeacon.com/politics/a-green-billionaires-dirty-money/

14 https://web.archive.org/web/20170514214807/https://www.opense-crets.org/industries/contrib.php?cycle=2016&ind=F03

15 https://web.archive.org/web/20180405013700/http://beneficialstate-bank.com/about-us/our-history

16 https://web.archive.org/web/20170514214807/https://www.opense-crets.org/industries/contrib.php?cycle=2016&ind=F03

17 https://web.archive.org/web/20171018042707/http://money.cnn.com/2017/10/17/news/george-soros-18-billion-open-society-founda-tions/index.html

18 http://archive.li/20qiv

19 http://archive.li/iMe77

20 https://web.archive.org/web/20180415051157/https://www.washingtonexaminer.com/news/watchdog-reveals-obama-administra-tion-provided-9-million-to-george-soros-political-activities-in-albania

21 https://web.archive.org/web/20180503125355/https://en.wikipedia.org/wiki/Michael_Bloomberg

22 https://web.archive.org/web/20180417095446/https://projects.pro-publica.org/nonprofits/organizations/205602483

23 https://web.archive.org/web/20180521174003/http://www.discover-thenetworks.org/printgroupProfile.asp?grpid=7945

24 https://web.archive.org/web/20180321223328/http://www.charlotteob-server.com/news/article9012470.html

25 Ibid.

26 https://web.archive.org/web/20161011081832/http://www.american-commitment.org:80/content/biggest-hypocrites-america

27 https://web.archive.org/web/20180520233317/https://podestaemails.blogspot.com/2016/10/herb-sandler-typhoid-mary-of-housing.html

28 https://web.archive.org/web/20180318012018/http://www.slate.com/articles/news_and_politics/press_box/2007/10/what_do_herbert_and_marion_sandler_want.html

29 https://web.archive.org/web/20170718165805/https://www.forbes.com/pictures/hhge45l/hillary-clintons-top-do/#5ac738fa2355

30 https://web.archive.org/web/20180416025356/https://www.theatlantic.com/health/archive/2018/04/sacklers-oxycontin-opioids/557525/

31 https://web.archive.org/web/20170602162208/http://freebeacon.com/issues/hillary-clintons-prescription-pill-problem-oxycontin-inventor-clinton-foundation-donor/

32 https://web.archive.org/web/20180520233538/https://capitalresearch.org/article/tides-legal-laundering-who-is-drummond-pike-one/

33 https://web.archive.org/web/20071019150250/http://www.discover-thenetworks.org/articles/Tides%20Foundation%20and%20Tides%20Center1.htm

34 https://web.archive.org/web/20180126140113/http://www.discover-thenetworks.org/funderProfile.asp?fndid=5184

35 Ibid.

36 https://web.archive.org/web/20180520233642/http://www.tides.org/wp-content/uploads/2017/06/Tides-2016-Audited-Financial-State-ments.pdf

37 http://archive.li/8AtBu

38 http://archive.li/Dk4wf

39 https://web.archive.org/web/20180421231333/https://pjmedia.com/election/soros-aligned-dem-donor-bankrolled-modern-marx-and-his-80-percent-income-tax/

40 https://web.archive.org/web/20170316064740/http://www.nber.org/papers/w22945.ack

Chapter 5

1   https://web.archive.org/web/20180520092545/https://www.pro-publica.org/about/

2   https://web.archive.org/web/20171207092221/http://dailycaller.com/2017/05/05/credibility-of-pulitzer-prize-takes-a-hit-by-reward-ing-propublicas-liberal-bias/

3   https://web.archive.org/web/20171016222458/http://discoverthenet-works.org/printgroupProfile.asp?grpid=7563

4   *Behind the Curtain*, p. 82.

5   https://web.archive.org/web/20180520073753/https://www.drugabuse.gov/related-topics/trends-statistics/overdose-death-rates

6   https://web.archive.org/web/20180213182606/
https://www.theguardian.com/us-news/2018/feb/13/
meet-the-sacklers-the-family-feuding-over-blame-for-the-opioid-crisis

7   https://web.archive.org/web/20180321155626/https://en.wikipedia.org/wiki/Southern_Poverty_Law_Center

8   https://web.archive.org/web/20180504081408/http://thefederalist.com/2017/05/17/12-ways-southern-poverty-law-center-scam-profit-hate-mongering/

9   Ibid.

10 https://web.archive.org/web/20180207194018/http://www.phi-lanthropyroundtable.org/topic/excellence_in_philanthropy/some_people_love_to_call_names

11 https://web.archive.org/web/20180520185849/
https://mediaequalizer.com/jeff-reynolds/2017/10/
against-social-media-censorship-do-conservatives-stand-a-chance

12 https://web.archive.org/web/20180422115149/https://www.lifesitenews.com/news/shadow-banning-how-twitter-secretly-censors-conserva-tives-without-them-even

13   https://web.archive.org/web/20180503115213/http://fortune.
      com/2018/01/19/facebook-twitter-news-feed-russia-ads/

14   https://web.archive.org/web/20180320232319/https://pjmedia.com/
      trending/twitter-admits-it-doesnt-understand-its-own-policies-after-
      suspending-pj-media-terror-expert/

15   https://web.archive.org/web/20180519063847/https://pjmedia.com/
      trending/pj-media-writer-suspended-twitter-just-hours-rush-lim-
      baugh-reads-article-lgbtqwtf/

16   https://web.archive.org/web/20180329234659/https://firstdraftnews.
      org/about/

17   https://web.archive.org/web/20180502171347/https://edition.cnn.
      com/2017/11/11/politics/podesta-group-mueller-investigation/index.
      html

18   https://web.archive.org/web/20170608222829/
      https://disobedientmedia.com/2017/06/
      fbi-documents-show-chinese-influence-in-bay-area-protest-groups/

19   https://archive.org/stream/AsianAmericanPoliticalAlliance/AsianA-
      mericanPoliticalAlliance04_djvu.txt

20   https://web.archive.org/web/20170608222829/
      https://disobedientmedia.com/2017/06/
      fbi-documents-show-chinese-influence-in-bay-area-protest-groups/

21   https://web.archive.org/web/20180513183722/http://foreignpolicy.
      com/2018/03/07/chinas-long-arm-reaches-into-american-campuses-
      chinese-students-scholars-association-university-communist-party/

22   Ibid.

23   Ibid.

24   https://web.archive.org/web/20180301144452/
      https://www.insidehighered.com/news/2018/02/15/
      fbi-director-testifies-chinese-students-and-intelligence-threats

25   https://web.archive.org/web/20180520235031/https://www.nationalre-
      view.com/2018/03/clinton-russia-collusion-evidence/

26   https://web.archive.org/web/20180324170616/https://science.house.
      gov/sites/republicans.science.house.gov/files/documents/SST%20

Staff%20Report%20-%20Russian%20Attempts%20to%20Influence%20
U.S.%20Domestic%20Energy%20Markets%20by%20Exploiting%20
Social%20Media%2003.01.18.pdf

27 Ibid., p 4

28 https://web.archive.org/web/20110901000000*/https://www.youtube.
com/watch?v=y3qkf3bajd4

29 https://web.archive.org/web/20180116070554/https://www.reuters.
com/article/us-usa-oil-record-shale-analysis/u-s-oil-industry-set-to-
break-record-upend-global-trade-idUSKBN1F50HV

30 https://web.archive.org/web/20180324170616/https://science.house.
gov/sites/republicans.science.house.gov/files/documents/SST%20
Staff%20Report%20-%20Russian%20Attempts%20to%20Influence%20
U.S.%20Domestic%20Energy%20Markets%20by%20Exploiting%20
Social%20Media%2003.01.18.pdf, p 7.

31 Ibid., p 13

32 Ibid., p 18

33 Ibid., p 21

34 https://web.archive.org/web/20180212023939/https://
www.washingtontimes.com/news/2017/jul/12/
klein-ltd-denies-funneling-russian-cash-to-us-envi/

Chapter 6

1 https://web.archive.org/web/20170517121549/https://oversight.house.
gov/wp-content/uploads/2014/01/Beale-Deposition.pdf

2 https://web.archive.org/web/20131111201903/http://www.truth-out.org/
opinion/item/19872-capitalism-and-the-destruction-of-life-on-earth-
six-theses-on-saving-the-humans

3 https://web.archive.org/web/20180324225340/http://www.claritypress.
com/Carter.html

4 Ibid.

5 https://web.archive.org/web/20180520200645/https://vimeo.
com/259400736

6   https://web.archive.org/web/20180510191110/https://monthlyreview.org/2008/09/01/the-u-s-media-reform-movement-going-forward/

7   https://web.archive.org/web/20140209042213/https://monthlyreview.org/2014/02/01/sharp-left-turn-media-reform-movement/

8   https://web.archive.org/web/20180221020413/http://www.discoverthenetworks.org/individualProfile.asp?indid=2227

9   https://web.archive.org/web/20180513161105/https://www.seattletimes.com/seattle-news/education/evergreen-professor-plans-to-sue-college-for-385-million/

10 https://web.archive.org/web/20170929140414/http://robertmcchesney.org:80/category/books/

11 https://web.archive.org/web/20180124223443/https://www.wsj.com/articles/SB10001424052748703886904576031512110086694

12 https://web.archive.org/web/20180517112441/http://archive2.mrc.org/articles/soros-ford-foundations-lavish-196-million-push-internet-regulations

13 https://web.archive.org/web/20180412103916/http://www.foxnews.com/opinion/2017/12/16/ending-net-neutrality-will-save-internet-not-destroy-it.html

14 https://web.archive.org/web/20180520235454/https://www.youtube.com/watch?v=0vh4Kp1TPWo

15 https://web.archive.org/web/20180328231507/https://marchforourlives.com/donate/

16 https://web.archive.org/web/20180510191110/https://monthlyreview.org/2008/09/01/the-u-s-media-reform-movement-going-forward/

17 https://web.archive.org/web/20180328231534/https://marchforourlives.com/faq/

18 https://web.archive.org/web/20180116075626/https://judithcurry.com/2015/02/25/conflicts-of-interest-in-climate-science/

19 https://web.archive.org/web/20171105120206/https://www.heartland.org/topics/climate-change/state-attorneys-general-launch-legal-attack-climate-realists/index.html

20 https://web.archive.org/web/20170722191947/
    https://www.heartland.org/news-opinion/news/
    justice-department-investigating-climate-skeptics

21 https://web.archive.org/web/20180513081601/https://www.ourchild-
    renstrust.org/

22 https://web.archive.org/web/20171204015529/https://www.theatlantic.
    com/magazine/archive/1997/02/the-capitalist-threat/376773/

Appendix

1   https://web.archive.org/web/20180514160909/http://www.discover-
    thenetworks.org/funderProfile.asp?fndid=5181

2   https://web.archive.org/web/20141203151626/https://www.theatlantic.
    com/magazine/archive/1997/02/the-capitalist-threat/376773/

3   https://web.archive.org/web/20180126140113/http://www.discover-
    thenetworks.org/funderProfile.asp?fndid=5184

4   https://web.archive.org/web/20171117120225/http://www.wweek.
    com:80/portland/article-3935-who-knew.html

5   https://web.archive.org/web/20161220192833/https://capitalresearch.
    org/article/blm-roots/

6   https://web.archive.org/web/20180330201605/https://www.indivisible.
    org/about-us/

7   https://web.archive.org/web/20180309045536/http://www.discover-
    thenetworks.org/funderprofile.asp?fndid=5184&category=79

8   https://web.archive.org/web/20180321171302/http://leftexposed.org/
    wp-content/uploads/2016/01/2014-Senate-Billionaire-Club-Report.pdf,
    p 54.

9   https://web.archive.org/web/20180309050039/http://www.discover-
    thenetworks.org/funderProfile.asp?fndid=5337

10 https://web.archive.org/web/20180520233956/https://www.hewlett.
    org/wp-content/uploads/2017/05/Hewlett-Foundation-2016-Audited-
    Financial-Statements.pdf

11 https://web.archive.org/web/20180520234049/https://www.fordfoundation.org/media/3666/2016-990pf-final-111417-website.pdf

12 https://web.archive.org/web/20180520234133/https://projects.propublica.org/nonprofits/organizations/131684331

13 https://web.archive.org/web/20180104052025/http://www.discoverthenetworks.org/funderProfile.asp?fndid=5176

14 Ibid.

15 https://web.archive.org/web/20180520234239/https://projects.propublica.org/nonprofits/organizations/131659629

16 https://web.archive.org/web/20180321171302/http://leftexposed.org/wp-content/uploads/2016/01/2014-Senate-Billionaire-Club-Report.pdf

17 Ibid., p 63

18 Ibid., p 13

19 https://web.archive.org/web/20171227194546/http://leftexposed.org/2016/08/environmental-grantmakers-association/

20 https://web.archive.org/web/20180205071053/http://leftexposed.org/2016/01/the-energy-foundation/

21 https://web.archive.org/web/20180520234513/https://capitalresearch.org/article/inside-the-seiu-funding-the-left/

ACKNOWLEDGMENTS

It would be impossible to thank everyone who helped me produce this book, or even those who tolerated me as I went through the process. For technical assistance and pointing me in the right direction, I want to thank Matt Margolis, Trevor Louden, Matthew Vadum, James Dellinger, Sarah Hoyt, and Chris Horner. Their assistance in research and in the technical aspects of writing was invaluable.

I want to thank my father, Ted, for the encouragement and the tolerance as I rushed to get this done while on a recent visit.

Big ups to my editor, David Bernstein, for his unwavering optimism, and faith in my ability to do this.

Thanks to that plucky band of patriots in the Oregon Tea Party, the toughest tea party in America. We talked for years about doing something like this, and now it's a reality. The support, suggestions, and encouragement from each leader helped me get to this point.

And most of all, thanks to my wife, Kathy, for the seemingly endless sacrifices and disruptions in our daily routine as I navigated this process. It wasn't always easy, but she never stopped believing in me.